A BIRDWATCHING GUIDE TO

FLORIDA

ARLEQUIN

ISBN 1 900159 55 4

First published 1997

Arlequin Press, 26 Broomfield Road, Chelmsford, Essex CM1 1SW
Telephone: 01245 267771

A catalogue record for this book is available.

CONTENTS

This book is dedicated to my wife Beryl who shares my love of North America, its wildlife and its people

FOREWORD by Bill Oddie

I didn't really want to go to Disneyworld, but my wife and daughter insisted. I had visions of hordes of 'resting' actors in character costumes, armies of gigantically overfed Americans, huge queues, crying babies, noisy rides, everything artificial, nothing natural and of course — worst of all — no birds! I warned my family of the consequences: "I won't be happy. I shall sulk. And then you won't be happy." How wrong I was. OK, there were queues and characters and crowds, but in fact the whole place was — and is — quite fantastically entertaining and enormous fun. More to the point though, there were — and are — birds. And not just Donald and his nephews. Real ones.

By breakfast time on the first day — after an hour's saunter along the river outside our Tree House Villa in the Disney Village — I had accumulated a holiday trip list of nigh on 40 species. These included at least half a dozen different herons and egrets, Barred and Great Horned Owls and a dazzling treeful of American warblers and vireos. This was followed by a day at the Epcot Centre — Pied Billed Grebe and Double Crested Cormorant — and Mickey's Birthday Parade — Turkey Vulture and Bald Eagle — and I was hooked on Florida.

I still am. Over the years, I have allowed my family to drag me back there many times. My only stipulation for giving in to this lack of imagination is that we visit at different seasons. This way I have experienced almost everything this gloriously productive state has to offer — birdwise that is — from cascades of Yellow Rumped Warblers in winter, to Nighthawks amongst the laser beams in late summer, to Swallow-tailed Kites in spring, and migrants at just about any time. I won't rattle on about the wondrous variety, beauty and tameness of Florida birds, because that's what this book is about to do! I will say, though, that there really can't be anywhere else in the world where the often completely disastrous combination of family holiday and birding can be so harmoniously achieved.

This book will certainly help you do just that. Or if you are solely birding, here is the necessary gen. And, of course, you don't HAVE to stay at Disneyworld . . . but you should at least visit. Have a nice day! (Or better still, a fantastic fortnight.)

Bill Oddie

BILL ODDIE

Acknowledgements
Thanks are particularly due to my good friend David Hosking who not only provided most of the photographs for this book and a section on photography but also encouraged me to take on the task as a venture with him. Thanks are also due to Michael Warren for the splendid cover. I am also indebted to my children Jeremy and Bronwen for coping with my obsession for birds, even on their holidays, and especially Jeremy who is now definitely hooked.

Author's Introduction

Birding abroad reaches new horizons year on year with most of the adventurous travelling widely in Europe and further afield in the quest for new species. Opportunities are sometimes limited if the prime reason for travelling widely is business or taking the family on holiday.

When my children were very young I selfishly chose holiday destinations where the birding was good and got up at dawn each day in order to satisfy my thirst for watching birds. The rest of the day belonged to the family. Florida is just the sort of destination I would select for a holiday if I still had young children. Many birders must be keen to visit the sunshine state for its wealth of bird life, but might be frustrated at the thought of taking the kids to Disneyworld every day and not getting a chance to get some lifers. Thoughts might stray to the horrors of shopping and sightseeing with so many birds to find.

Well! Worry no more. This guide is aimed precisely at you. The opportunities to combine some fantastic birding whilst giving the family every chance to enjoy Disneyworld, the beach and shopping etc are enormous. This book concentrates on describing some of the best sites close to Orlando and Miami, all of which can be reached with comparative ease. These sites provide a good chance of finding most of the Florida specialities depending of course on when you time your visit.

This book seeks to encourage you to travel to the listed sites, but frankly, you can see good birds almost anywhere. Even as you touch down at an airport all is possible. To give you an example: as I arrived at Orlando on one occasion I glanced from the window and immediately noted Anhinga, Snowy and Great Egrets on a patch of water and most surprising of all an Osprey rising from the pool carrying a large fish. Even shopping downtown sees birds in any patch of trees; Red-headed Woodpeckers attract attention along with Northern Mockingbirds and Mourning Doves. In Miami do not be surprised to come across flocks of Canary-winged Parakeets or Common Mynahs.

Driving around the countryside also brings more and more; close-cropped lawns south of Kissimmee may attract Sandhill Cranes and roadside ditches attract egrets, herons and even Wood Storks. Roadside wires attract Belted Kingfishers and Red-shouldered and Broad-winged Hawks.

There is so much to see even without a great deal of effort.

The sites in this guide are very much based on personal preference. If you want to travel more widely in Florida you really must get a copy of the invaluable "A Birder's Guide To Florida" by Bill Pranty and published by the American Birding Association.

When to visit

February to April would probably produce the biggest list of species, but November/ December can be excellent and some outstanding deals on flights can be had just before Christmas. Avoid midsummer as heat and insects will put a stop to much birding.

Getting around

As in most places in the United States everything, including birding, is based around the motor car. Car hire is fairly cheap but insurance can be expensive. Beware of flydrive deals which promise a car free. The latter generally means you have to wait for hours sometimes to get your car and then you find it is the smallest model. You then find yourself paying for an upgrade as well as for 'special state handling' charges and insurance. It can actually be cheaper to take the cheap flight and make your own car arrangements. Car hire companies now do not put their names on cars or have specific number plates. In other words it is not easy now for your car to be instantly recognised as a tourist vehicle.

The American road system generally follows a series of parallel grids and once you have mastered this driving is easy. Most vehicles have automatic transmission which makes life easier still. Many main highways and bridges charge tolls, so have a few dollars handy.

Road maps

In conjunction with this book I recommend Rand McNally Regional Maps.

Where to stay

There are so many motels and hotels in the state that you can take your pick. Many package holidays from UK will include a hotel. If you are moving around the motel chains can be excellent. Self-catering accommodation can also be a convenient method, especially if you have small children.

Weather

Can be very variable but mostly warm and sunny. From May to October temperatures can be very hot with high humidity. At other times temperatures vary, but days are normally sunny although it does rain sometimes. Florida residents freeze and headlines are made if the temperature drops below 20°C.

Dangerous animals

Alligators are numerous in wetlands and often seen. If you respect the animals and keep your distance you will have no problems at all. Indeed you will be lucky to see an Alligator move. It is absolutely illegal to feed Alligators as this creates nuisance animals which sadly usually have to be shot. Remember Alligators cannot easily distinguish between your hand and the piece of bread so stick to the rules.

Racoons are a common sight in some areas and in particular some parks. Do not feed them or try to pet them as they can be carriers of rabies.

There are six species of poisonous snake in Florida which are indicated in the checklist at the back of this book. For details of field identification consult *Peterson's Field Guide to the Reptiles and Amphibians of Eastern/Central North America.* You will be very lucky to see any snake as long as you stick to marked trails and paths but should you encounter one keep your distance. Do not attempt to touch any snake or to act in a provocative manner.

Biting insects

You should always carry effective insect repellant. Apart from the Snake Bight Trail in the Everglades mosquito problems are low in winter.

Crime

Much has been written about Florida and its dangers. My experience suggests that as long as you keep well clear of downtown Miami you should not have any trouble. If you concentrate on visiting the areas mentioned in this book you will be unlikely to suffer any inconvenience except deciding on which bird to look at next.

Florida Birdline

Ring the Florida Birding Report on 941-657-4442 for statewide information. If in Miami call 912-244-9190. In the Lower Keys call 305-294-3438.

Plate 1. *Coniferous woodland including Slash Pine still hold Red-cockaded Woodpecker and Bachman's Sparrow.* David Hosking

Plate 2. *The stands of Giant Cypress are a favourite haunt of Barred Owls.* David Hosking

Plate 3. *Loxahatchee National Wildlife Refuge – Snail Kite site.* Derek Moore

Plate 4. *The wide open grasslands of the Everglades.* David Hosking

Plate 5. *The impressive boardwalk of the Anhinga Trail.* Derek Moore

Plate 6. *Fairchild Gardens, favoured by Ruby-throated Hummingbirds.* Derek Moore

Plate 7. *Matheson Hammock a prime site in South Miami.* Derek Moore

Plate 8. *Few birdwatchers get as far as Prairie Lakes National Park.* Derek Moore

Plate 9. *The Ding Darling National Wildlife Refuge is a birdwatcher's paradise.* David Hosking

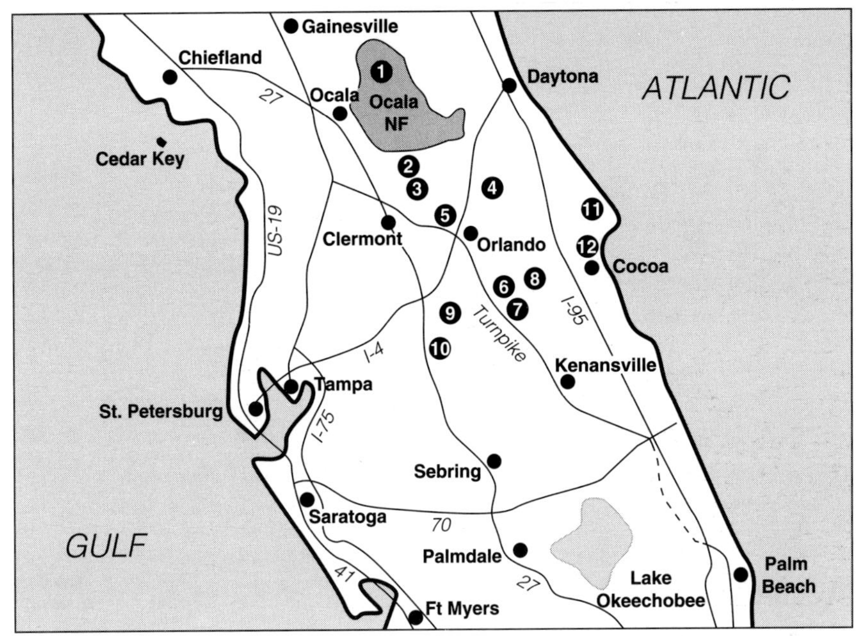

Orlando area.

Birding from Orlando

1. The Ocala Forest

This extensive coniferous woodland lies about an hour's drive to the north-west of Orlando. This National Forest covers an area of nearly 400,000 acres and consists mostly of Slash Pine, but there are isolated stands of Long-leaved Pine which is the habitat of the scarce Red-cockaded Woodpecker. Look for the telltale marks of small holes and running sap which is made by these birds. Other species found in these areas include Pine Warbler, Bachman's Sparrow and Brown-headed Nuthatch. Summer sees more species in the forest and these include Swallow-tailed Kite, Acadian Warbler, Summer Tanager and Prothonotary Warbler. The areas of oak scrub around the forest contain the Florida Scrub Jay.

The forest is vast and it is therefore advisable to stop at the Forest Service Visitor Centre at Silver Springs to ask for the latest information on the Red-cockaded Woodpecker. Forest staff often mark trees which the birds are currently using. The most favoured areas are around Alexander Springs and Salt Springs.

2. Lake Woodruff National Wildlife Refuge

Join US-17 north of Orlando and continue on to De Leon Springs. Head west on Retta Street and then left into Grand Avenue. Look for a right turn into Mud Lake Road and carry straight on to the car park.

The reserve is a series of ponds surrounded by raised banks on which you can walk freely. There is also some woodland which is worth searching for passerines. In summer Swallow-tailed Kites are here as well as Bald Eagles. This site is outstanding for wetland species and one of the best for obtaining close views of Limpkin. Osprey is regular and other raptors noted here include Cooper's Hawk and Red-shouldered Hawk. Great and Snowy Egrets, Green Herons and Little Blue and Tri-coloured Herons are easy to find.

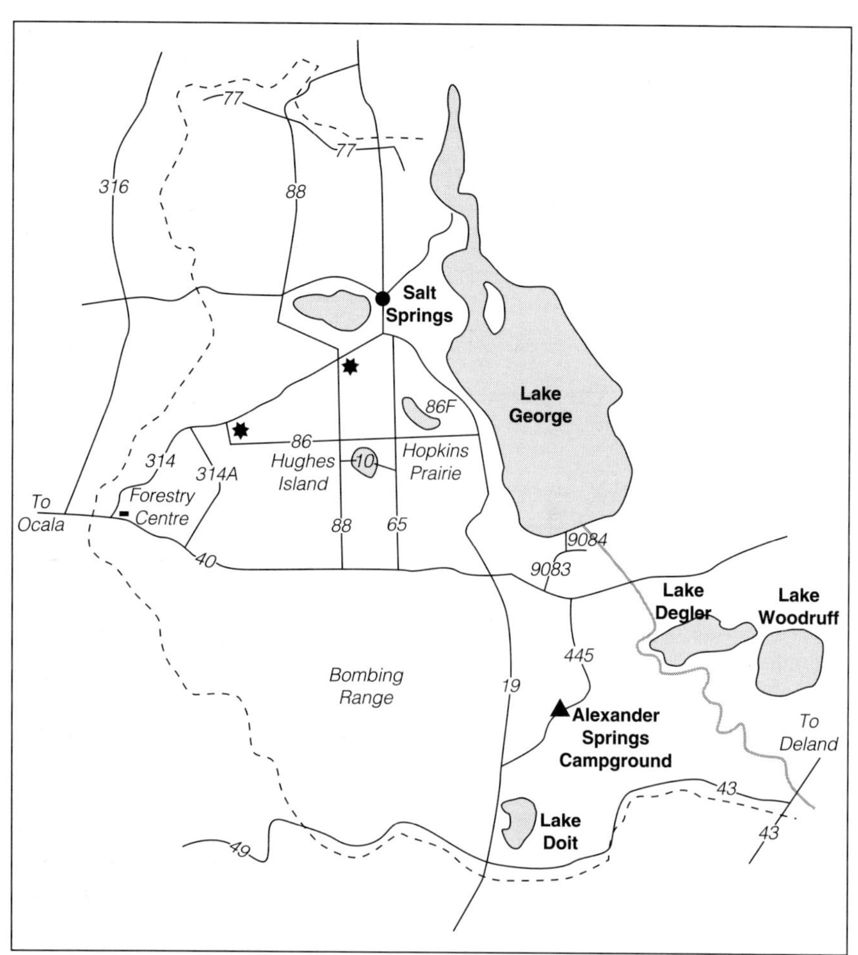

Site 1. Ocala National Forest.

Waterfowl are represented by hordes of noisy American Coots as well as ducks such as Blue-winged Teal and Ring-necked Duck. Anhingas stand snake-like on dyke banks and both Glossy and White Ibises abound. Winter sees both Caspian and Forster's Terns fishing over the open water.

3. Blue Springs State Recreation Area

South of Lake Woodruff on US-17. Follow signs west on French Avenue to reach the park. Good in winter for large roosting flocks of grackles and blackbirds. Water birds include Anhinga and Double-crested Cormorant. The main reason to come here is not for birds at all but for an unforgettable confrontation with Manatees. Large numbers winter in the fantastically clear waters of the stream and can be viewed early morning from a wooden pier from December until February. One such visit by the author in December revealed 18 animals all within 20 metres.

4. Sanford

There are a series of lakes along SR-46 all of which are very productive and suitable for

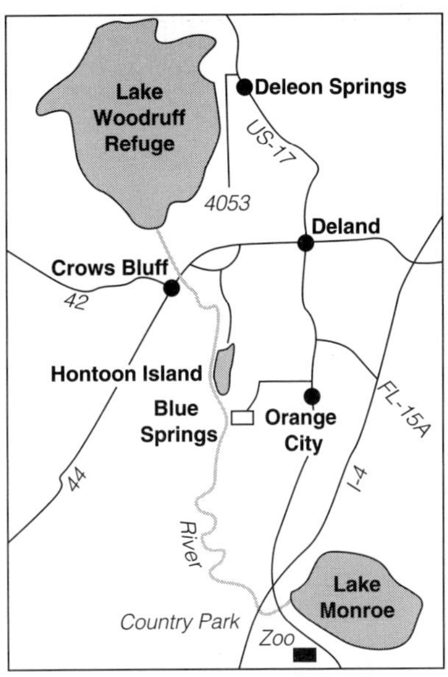

Sites 2&3. Lake Woodruff & Blue Springs State Recreation Area.

somebody who is pressed for time. Stop first at Lake Jessup Inlet where there is a substantial marsh. In summer Least Bitterns may be found here and Mottled Ducks are residents of this area. Winter sees the arrival of flocks of wildfowl, American Coots and Pied-billed Grebes. Swallow-tailed Kite occurs in summer. Mullet Lake Park is found by turning left at Osceala Road, turning left again into the park. This tree-decked hammock is excellent for finding passerines which include resident Carolina Wrens, Pileated Woodpeckers and in winter warblers such as Black and White and Parula. Check the lake for waterfowl.

The wetland grassy areas in the park often hold shorebirds and herons as well as Sandhill Cranes and Wood Storks. Returning to the SR-46 stop at Lake Harney to check for White Pelicans in winter.

5. Zellwood and Wekiwa Springs State Park

You find this area by driving US-441 on Laughlin Road. Just north of Zellwood you find Jones Road on the left which is a good access. Canal Road found by a sign for Living Carpet Sod and Nursery is also worth trying. Canal Road is on the south side of Jones Road. The farms are private so respect this when looking at birds. Beware of very wet roads or you might get stuck.

Probably only worth visiting in late summer. The area is a series of vegetable farms where the fields are flooded in August to remove pests. At this time shorebirds and other waterfowl abound and include several species difficult to find elsewhere. Mottled Duck and Fulvous Whistling Duck can be present as well as Glossy Ibis and Black-necked Stilt which nests. Many shorebird species occur including the elusive Buff-breasted Sandpiper and rarities occur regularly. Call Mr Giles Van Dyne 407-886-1932 before visiting. Wekiwa Springs State Park is worth a visit. Migrating passerines and Limpkin occur.

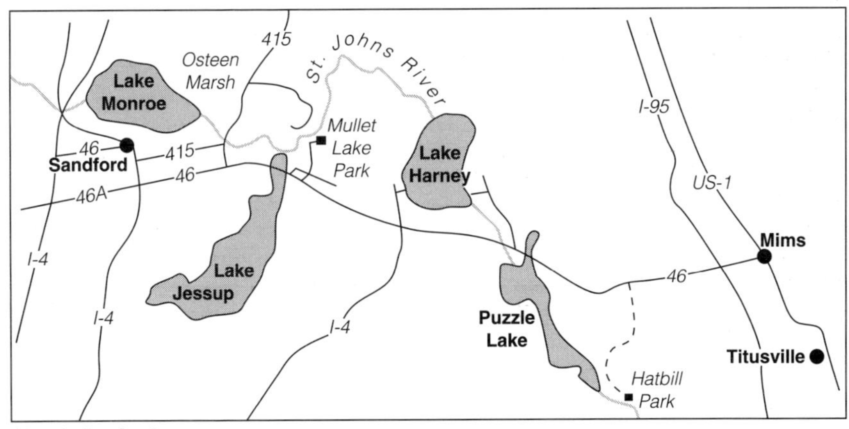

Site 4. Sanford area.

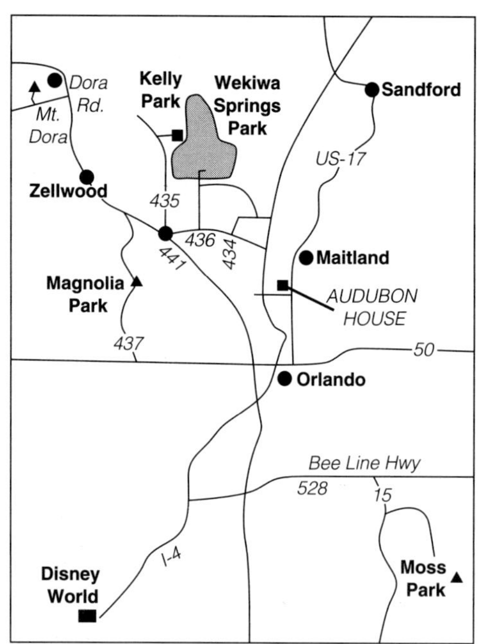

Site 5. Zellwood & Wekina Springs Park.

6. Lake Tohopekaliga

One of the best areas south of Orlando. You drive south of Kissimmee on US-17 turning left on SR-531. The lake runs parallel to this road on your left.

The fields on either side of the road can have Sandhill Cranes and in the early morning Wild Turkeys. Driving some way down the road look for a gravelled track called Mac Overstreet on your left. This is a private road but birders seem to be tolerated. Entering the area you will note grasslands with cattle and these are worth checking for sparrows, Sandhill Cranes, Cattle Egrets and Bald Eagles. Drive on to the belt of trees where you can leave the vehicle. You can wander freely along the shore but views of the open water may be frustratingly few. Having said this the birding here can be marvellous.

Shallows by the reedy edges hold Tri-coloured Heron, Little Blue Heron, Glossy Ibis, White Ibis and American Coots. Look carefully at flights of wildfowl for Fulvous Whistling Duck as well as American Black Duck. Sandhill Cranes can be heard and seen and Ospreys and Bald Eagles regularly overfly the area. This is an excellent place for Fish Crows.

Contining further south you can visit the Reedy Creek reserve which you find by turning right onto Poinciana Boulevard. This reserve is only open after 10am on Saturdays and Sundays. There is a series of boardwalks in a wooded swamp where Wood Storks, Anhinga and maybe Barred Owls can be found.

Coming back to the SR-531 cross straight over and head for Southport. After a while there is a large rubbish tip on your left. Look from the road for Turkey and Black Vultures. Continuing on you pass extensive grasslands interspersed with trees. Check the area carefully for raptors including Crested Caracara which often sit on the tops of isolated palms. Sandhill Cranes, Loggerhead Shrikes and flocks of grackles and blackbirds also occur here.

Reaching the end of the road turn into the marina car park. Here you can view the lake and also take a ride in a windboat which kids will simply love. The latter is an excellent way of seeing birds as long as you can persuade the driver to slow down and even stop occasionally. There is an obsession with showing customers Alligators but with a little persuasion birding can be great. Look out for large flocks of Double-crested Cormorants, Anhinga, Purple Gallinule, Belted Kingfisher, Forsters Tern, Bald Eagle and Green Heron.

Heading back turn left on SR-531 and check out the sides of the road in Poinciana where Wood Storks and herons feed in the ditches and Red-shouldered Hawks watch from power lines. The SR-531 ends to the south at The Scrub Jay Trail in the Disney Wilderness Preserve. This is worth walking for Florida Scrub Jays, Summer Tanager and Bald Eagle.

7. Lake Kissimmee State Park

Another marvellous area which can easily accommodate a whole day. The park is reached by heading east on FL-60 from Lake Wales. After a while turn left on Boy Scout Road (just after the camp gate look for Florida Scrub Jay on your right) and then right on Camp Mark Road. There is a small charge to enter.

There is a large parking lot and toilets and picnic area. Birds occur everywhere even near the parking lot. The tall trees around the buildings and car park can be good for passerines. Small flocks include warblers with Yellow-throated as well as Red-breasted and Pileated Woodpecker. The wooden jetty is great for Belted Kingfisher and fishing herons.

Several Bald Eagles nest in the park and are a regular sight as are Crested Caracaras. If you walk to the far end of the parking lot you can climb the lookout tower for great views of the area including the lake. Look out for Swallow-tailed Kite in summer.

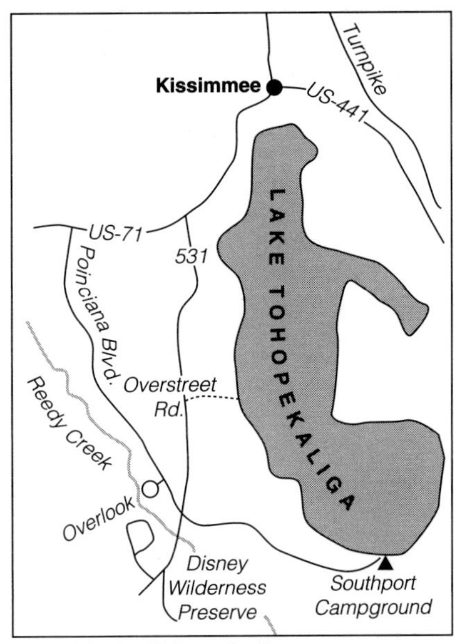

Site 6. Lake Tohopekaliga.

There are a number of trails that can be walked. Leaving the parking lot you can follow signs to the 'Cow Camp'. Here volunteers behave and speak just as the first settlers did whilst tending their cattle. The family will love this and however hard you try to talk of present day things the 'cowhands' will keep on talking as if you were there a hundred years ago. You can then follow a couple of extensive trails in open country and pine woods. Here Loggerhead Shrikes and Eastern Meadowlarks occur in the grassy areas. Under the pines watch out for the scarce and elusive Bachman's Sparrow. The trees might have Eastern Bluebird, Rufous-sided Towhee, Red-headed Woodpecker and Brown-headed Nuthatch.

The trail on the other side of the road to the 'Cow Camp' starts in very wooded country and is excellent for passerines. In summer Parulas and Summer Tanagers breed and in winter large foraging flocks can include Pine Warbler, Black and White Warbler, Palm Warbler, White-eyed and Solitary Viroes and Red-bellied Woodpecker. Walking on you can get reasonable views of the lake and open country where more excellent views of Bald Eagles and vultures will be easy. Watch out for amazing Armadillos.

8. Prairie Lakes Preserve

A bit more remote than previous sites but worth a visit if you have time. The reserve is part of the Three Lakes Wildlife Management Area and is found on the east side of Lake Kissimmee near Kenansville. You find it by driving north from SR-60 on US-441 and then left after 13 miles on the SR-523 for a further six miles to the entrance. You drive along dirt roads and can really explore at will. Your first stop might be where you cross open water over a small bridge. There is a parking lot on your right. The culvert under the road provided the author with the best views ever of Limpkin. The birds seemed used to people and allowed themselves to be watched and photographed from less than 15 metres.

Just follow the roads to various points where you can look over the lake. Do not be put off if you see nobody about; the more you explore the more you will see. The woodlands had many flocks of birds during one December visit. They included Yellow-rumped and Palm Warblers. Large flocks of American Robins, Blue-grey Gnatcatchers as well as Pileated and Downy Woodpeckers. The open water revealed large numbers of Blue-

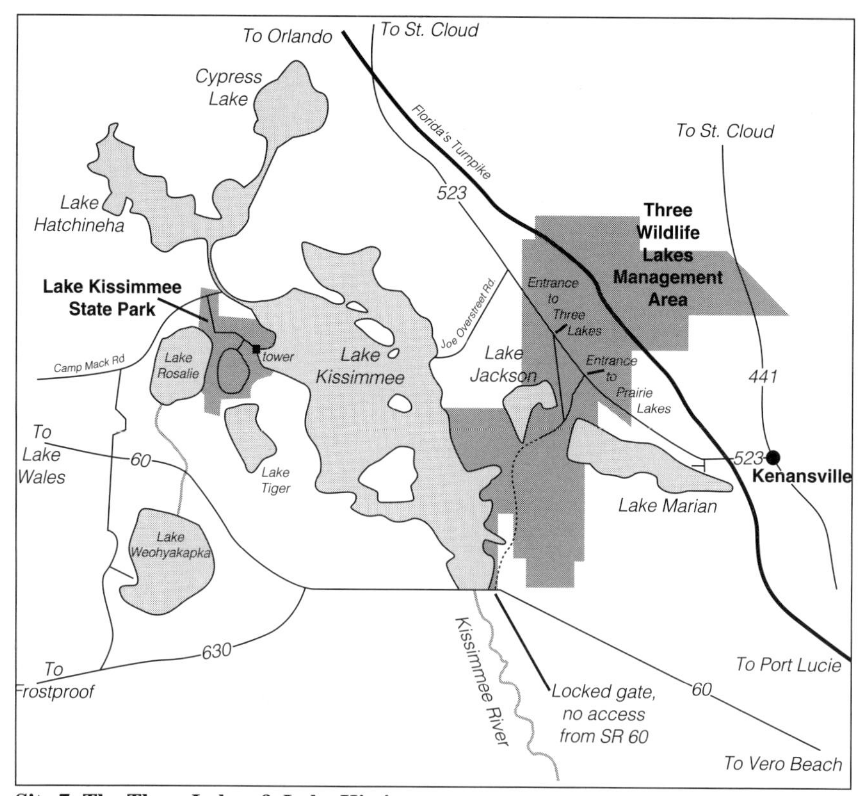

Site 7. The Three Lakes & Lake Kissimmee.

winged Teal, Anhingas, Green, Tri-coloured and Little Blue Herons and also Great and Snowy Egrets. Black and Turkey Vultures were numerous and Bald Eagles, Northern Harrier, Sharp-shinned Hawk, American Kestrel and Red-shouldered Hawks were also noted. Great views of Alligators, Raccoons and Armadillos completed a splendid day. Coming back to the SR-523 go north and turn down Joe Overstreet Road for Wild Turkey, Burrowing Owl and if you are lucky the introduced Whooping Cranes.

9. Lake Placid

The area east of Lake Placid is extremely productive and will certainly add much to a birding trip if you have time. Head east on SR-70 from US-27 six miles south of the town. The remaining prairie areas should be searched for Crested Caracara, Sandhill Crane and the amusing Burrowing Owl. Florida Scrub Jays are here and Glossy Ibises can also be found. There has unfortunately been much planting of citrus crops in recent years but there is still much to look for. The Shira Road which is reached by turning left onto the SR-29 and then right following a small loop. Here Swallow-tailed Kites nest in summer as well as Barred Owl and Yellow-billed Cuckoo. In winter rarities such as Scissor-tailed Flycatcher have been found.

If you return to SR-70 and head east you will find many other good habitats of grasslands, wet areas and Cabbage Palms. These are all worth checking. Burrowing Owls prefer well drained sandy soils with a short grass covering. The area around Brighton is especially good for these birds. Check mounds and fence posts.

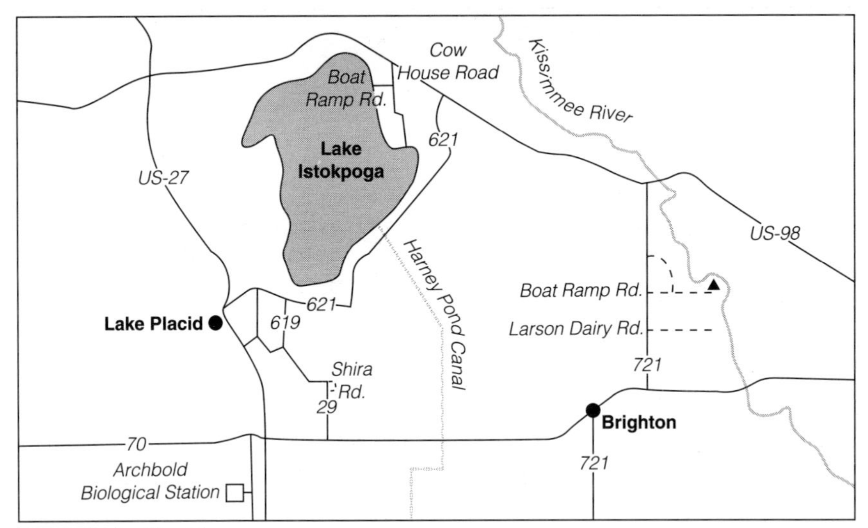

Site 9. Lake Placid.

10. Old Venus

This area refers to an isolated stand of Long-leafed Pines which have somehow survived the destruction of the past. To find this spot you head south on US-27 turning west on SR-731 and then north on Old SR-8 until you find the dirt Sheppard Road (also called Boothill Road). The pines are on the left. Red-cockaded Woodpecker may still occur here as well as Pine Warbler, Bachman's Sparrow and Brown-headed Nuthatch.

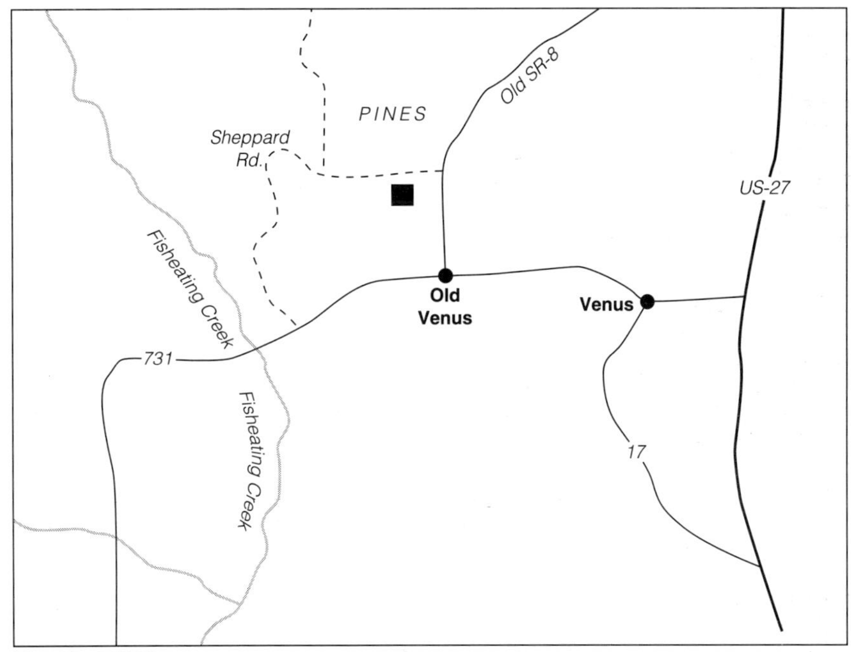

Site 10. Old Venus.

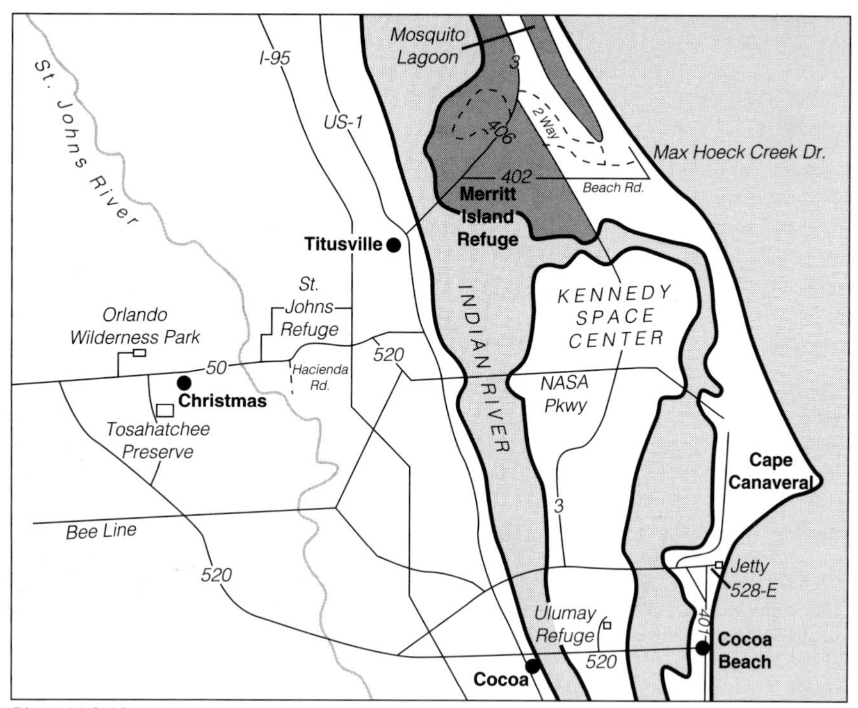

Sites 11&12. Merritt Island.

11. Merritt Island — Black Point Wildlife Drive

If travelling from Orlando go east on any route until you reach US-1 near Titusville then turn east on SR-406. Heading over the bridge pause by parking lots for views of gulls, terns and Brown Pelicans. It is also possible to see dolphins from here.

Keep left at Beach Road moving on to the entrance to the Black Point Wildlife Drive on your left. You can pick up a leaflet to this loop drive as you enter. This is an excellent place to experience the wildlife of this magnificent reserve. There are various stopping points where very close views can be obtained. Around halfway there is a parking lot and a short walk to an observation tower. From here the really energetic can do a long circular hike lasting about two hours.

The author visited this area twice recently in December and recorded the following: White Pelican, Roseate Spoonbill, Reddish Egret, Anhinga, Glossy and White Ibises and Wood Stork. Large numbers of wildfowl included Snow Geese, Hooded Mergansers, Pintail, American Wigeon, Green-winged and Blue-winged Teal. Shorebirds were present in large numbers and included American Avocets, Stilt Sandpiper, Willets, Marbled Godwits, Lesser and Greater Yellowlegs, Short-billed Dowitchers and Ruddy Turnstones. Searching the muddy ditches produced Virginia and King Rail. Bonapartes Gulls, Royal, Caspian and Forsters Terns and Ospreys were also very obvious. Alligators are common in the roadside ditches.

Coming back to the Beach Road drive east to the Visitor Centre. In winter you will pass open water with thousands more wildfowl and herons as well as excellent views of rockets on the Cape Canaveral skyline (great for the kids: a visit to the Kennedy Space Center is easy from this area). Watch out for Florida Scrub Jay which occurs on the drive down to the ocean. In summer the beaches are crowded but out of season worth a look. Northern Gannets are offshore in winter and flocks of gulls and terns together with Black Skimmers loaf on the sand.

Plate 10. *The tangled mangroves are home to the elusive Mangrove Cuckoo.* David Hosking

Plate 11. *The coastal waters of Biscayne Bay are home to many gulls, terns and shorebirds.* Derek Moore

Plate 12. *Man's presence does not deter Burrowing Owls.* David Hosking

Plate 13. *Merritt Island with the rockets of Cape Canaveral behind.* Derek Moore

***Plate 14.** The magnificent Bald Eagle is a great feature of Florida birding.* David Hosking

Plate 15. *Turkey Vulture is one of the common scavengers of the area.*

David Hosking

Plate 16. *Black Vultures are generally less common than Turkey Vultures.*

Derek Moore

Plate 17. *Ospreys are numerous and even nest on roadside poles.*

David Hosking

Plate 18. *The Florida race of the Red-shouldered Hawk is commonly seen perched on roadside wires.*

David Hosking

12. Merritt Island — Cocoa; Ulumay Refuge and Jetty Park

To find Ulumay Refuge go east on SR-520 from US-1 at Cocoa. Turn north on Sykes Creek Parkway and after crossing the first bridge turn left into the Refuge. There is a small parking lot and from there you can walk freely around the dykes. This is said to be a good site for Black Rail — so Good Luck! The many pools and creeks play host to Mottled Duck, Roseate Spoonbill, Brown Pelican, herons, ibises and Wood Stork. Osprey and Bald Eagle are regularly overhead and Common Ground Doves frequent the grassy paths.

Jetty Park is further east and reached by heading for Port Canaveral on SR-A1A. Jetty Park is on the right. At first you might wonder if there is any point stopping here. Well, if you avoid peak times there can be birds. The beach often has loafing gulls, Royal Terns and Black Skimmers. Shorebirds include Willet and Sanderling and Gannets are offshore in winter. Around the campsite you should look for Florida Scrub Jay and Smooth-billed Ani.

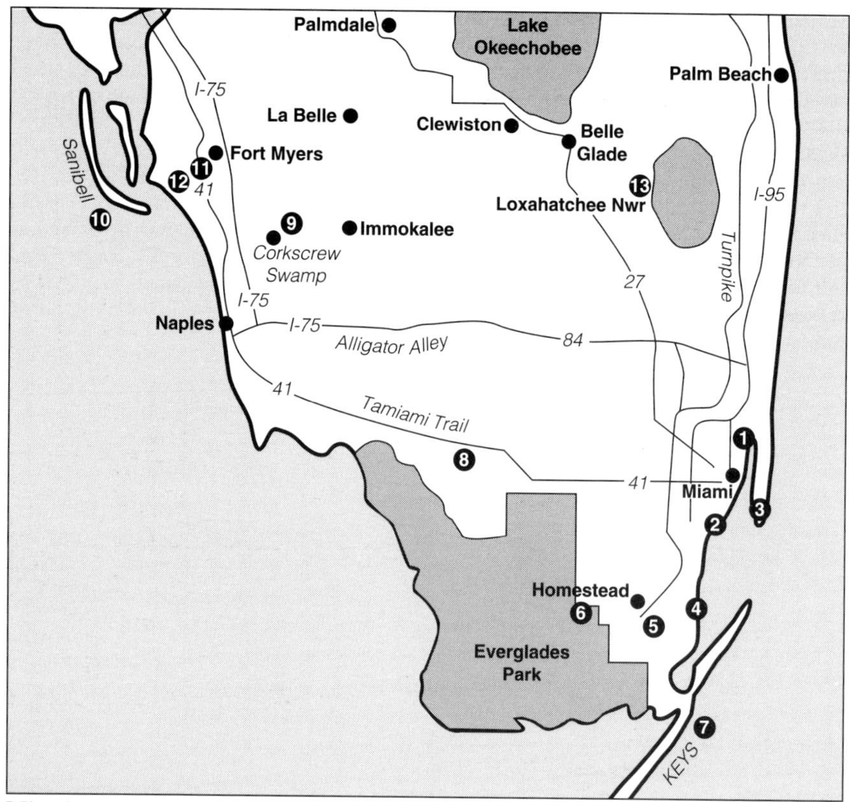

Miami area.

Birding from Miami

Any of the city parks can be excellent for birding but the following two are particularly good and very safe areas.

1. Greynolds Park, North Miami

To find this hotspot you drive north on Biscayne Boulevard US-1 to NE-172nd Street. You need the west entrance so turn left and cross the tracks and then right. Park in the first area after turning left. Follow the road up to the tower then turn left and go on to the golf course then go left by the greens to seats across from the rookery.

Greynolds Park is famous for the introduced Scarlet Ibises. Now so interbred with White Ibises that most representatives are only pink. Indeed some recent works place the Scarlet Ibis as a race of White Ibis. Also nesting on the islands are Anhingas, herons, Cattle Egrets and Double-crested Cormorants. The best time to visit the park is in the evening when the birds fly in to roost.

Check other areas out for Spot-breasted Oriole. The large flowering tree near the clubhouse on the golf course is a good bet.

2. Matheson Hammock County Park

To find this excellent site head for Coral Gables on US-1 and turn off south down Cutler Road. The Park entrance is on the left.

There are five main birding options:

a) Go through the marina area to the beach where there is a parking lot near a swimming pool. Early in the morning is best when few people are here. Excellent point for seeing Brown Pelicans and Black Skimmers. Also shorebirds, gulls and terns are regular with Royal Terns common. Fish Crows are regular here and check the flocks of grackles and blackbirds in winter for Rusty or Brewer's Blackbird.

b) On entering the park follow the road on until it ends by mangroves looking out to the ocean from a small beach. The shoreline attracts shorebirds such as Killdeer, Semipalmated Plover, Short-billed Dowitcher, Willet and many more. White Ibises, Little Blue Herons and Great Egrets feed nearby and Black Skimmers and Brown Pelicans fish here. Search the trees for passerines especially Yellow-throated Warblers.

c) Park in the spaces at the entrance of the park and just wander around the formal gardens and woodlands. Wintering passerines have included Cape May, Black and White, Yellow-rumped and Palm Warblers; Solitary, White-eyed and Yellow-throated Vireos. The pond attracts herons including Yellow-crowned Night Heron and Green-backed Heron. Common Ground Doves are regular and feral Hill Mynahs and escaped parrots should be looked for.

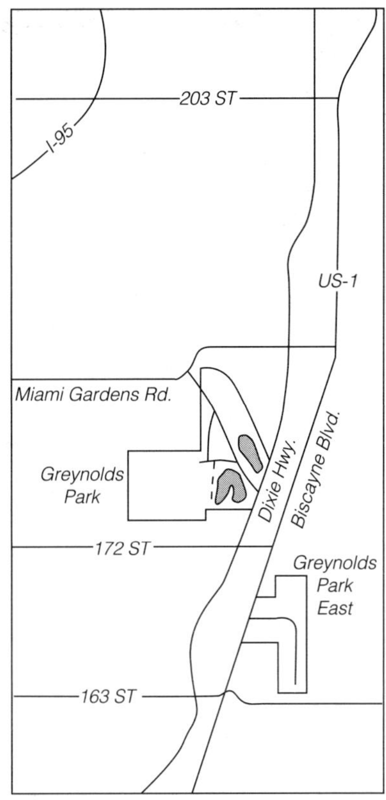

Site 1. Greynolds Park.

d) Park near the entrance but cross Cutler Road to enter a trail which leads through a large Hammock and then into more open grassy areas with woodland. Even though some books tell you otherwise this is one of the best places to find White-crowned Pigeon in winter. The author found five very obliging in December 1989. Large numbers of Turkey Vultures also roost here but there are also good opportunities for finding passerines. Carolina Wren is resident here as is Pileated Woodpecker. Look for warblers in winter which have included Parula and American Redstart.

e) Fairchild Tropical Gardens are next door to the Park and can be just as good. Most of the bird species will be similar but Ruby-throated Hummingbirds are a feature in winter feeding at many of the flowering shrubs.

3. Bill Baggs Park

You find this site by crossing to Key Biscayne and heading to the southern tip. Sadly the hurricane of 1992 has destroyed many of the trees in what was formerly a great area for migrants. The park is being replanted using native species so the future looks good and therefore a visit might be worthwhile. Many Caribbean rarities have turned up here in the past. Raptors are regular and include Peregrines and Cooper's Hawks.

4. Biscayne National Park

The best way to get a feel of this area is to visit Convoy Point which is found by driving south on US-1 and turning east on North Canal Drive which ends at the Park. Just walk around the car park to see lots of Brown Pelicans. Walk out along the small

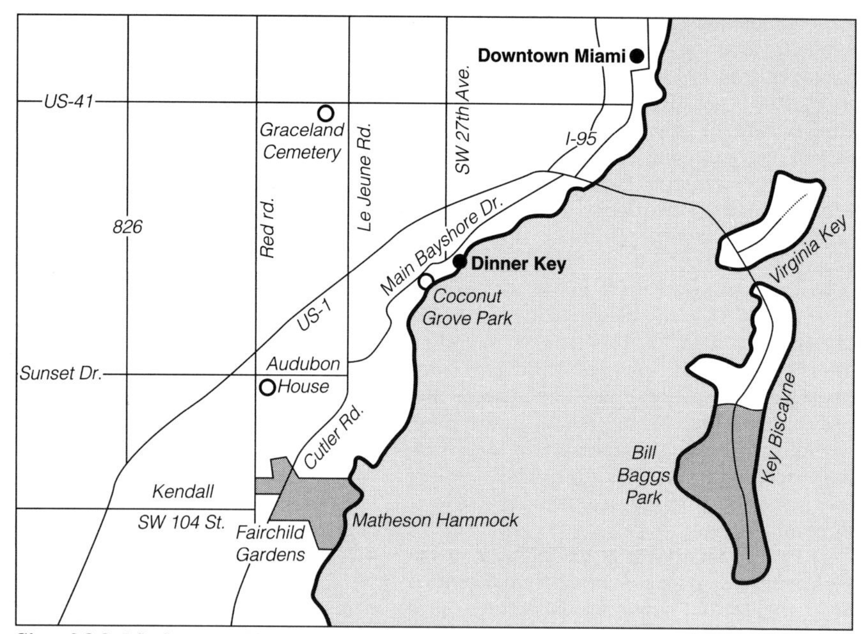

Sites 2&3. Mathewson Hammock and Bill Baggs Park.

jetty/breakwater for Black Skimmers, Royal and Sandwich Terns and shorebirds.

You can hire a boat to take you out to explore the area or merely buy a ticket for the glass-bottomed boat to explore the coral reef. The latter will enable you to get close to wintering Red-breasted Mergansers and Northern Gannets as well as residents like Brown Pelicans and Magnificent Frigate Birds.

If you can arrange to visit Elliot Key in summer you may find nesting White-crowned Pigeons and Grey Kingbirds. On the mainland the shoreline mangroves have summer breeding Black-whiskered Vireo and Mangrove Cuckoo.

Check out the trees and bushes around the parking area for flocks of small birds in winter. Red-bellied Woodpeckers, Pine, Prairie and Palm Warblers are regular as well as Yellowthroat. Stay in the evening for spectacular flypasts of herons going to roost.

5. Homestead Area

There are a number of interesting sites in the town of Homestead which is just south of Miami along US-1.

Castello Hammock was severely damaged in the hurricanes of the early nineties but is probably still worth a visit. You drive west along Hainlin Mill Drive between US-1 and SR-997 and find the area on SW 162nd Avenue. A children's nature study and visitor centre was totally destroyed by the hurricane but access is still possible and vital bird feeders are still operating at the time of writing. In winter Painted Buntings and White-winged Doves attend the feeders as well as other species. A large roost of Turkey and Black Vultures occurs and Smooth-billed Anis can be found in surrounding shrubbery. Both Yellow-billed and Mangrove Cuckoo have been found here in summer.

The Fruit and Spice Park is open 9am-5pm daily and is worth a quick visit especially to look for hummingbirds. Ruby-throated is regular and Rufous has been seen in autumn and winter. The Park is on SW 187th Avenue at the junction of coconut Palm Drive (SW 248th Street) and Redland Road (SW 187th Avenue).

The small airfield at Homestead (not to be confused with Homestead Air Force Base)

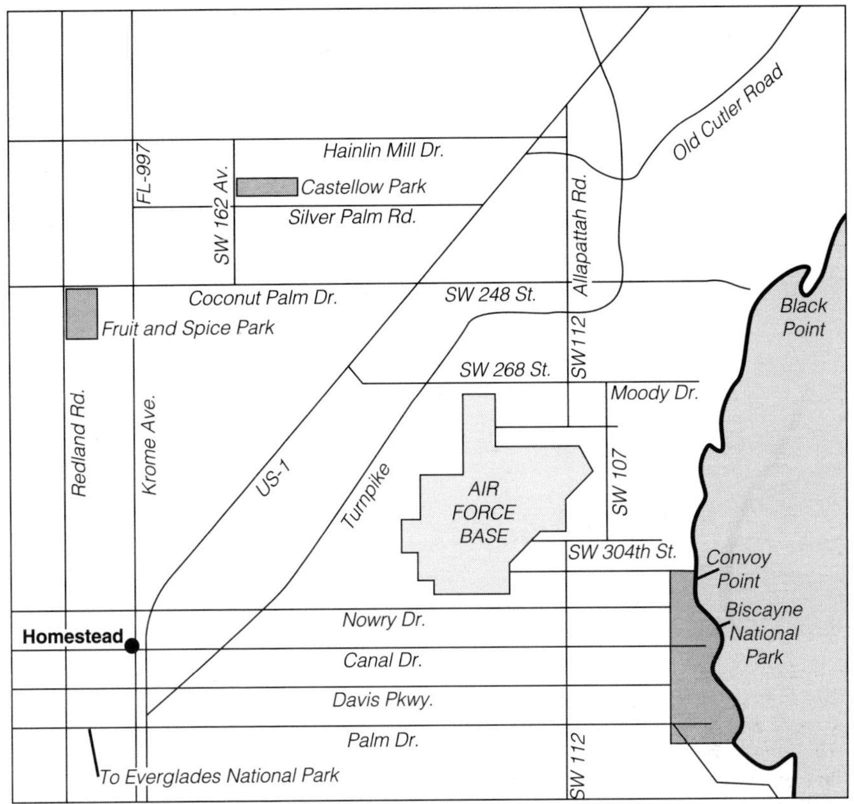

Sites 4&5. Biscayne National Park and Homestead area.

is another must. The flat grassy runways are home to many nesting Burrowing Owls and really close views can be obtained. Birdwatchers are welcomed but please do watch out for moving aircraft.

6. Everglades National Park

The biggest attraction for visitors whether interested in wildlife or not. The best plan is to enter via the Main Visitors Center which is reached on the SR-9336 west of Homestead. You can buy a weekly permit here as well as maps and bird lists and contemplate the drive all the way down to Flamingo stopping off at various key places.

Stay awhile around the Visitor Centre searching nearby vegetations for passerines and woodpeckers then enter the Park proper. Your first stop should be at Taylor Slough where you will get your first real look at the vast open spaces of the wet grassland interspersed with well wooded hammocks. If you are lucky you might catch a glimpse of the Cape Sable race of the Seaside Sparrow, but do not count on it as they are incredibly secretive. It is best to move on fairly quickly to the Royal Palm centre and the famous Anhinga Trail.

Once on the amazing raised boardwalk the birding is absolutely fantastic. As you would expect you can almost touch Anhingas as well as Great Blue, Tri-coloured, Little Blue and Green Herons. Search the thicker cover for American and Least Bitterns and both Black-crowned and Yellow-crowned Night Herons. Purple Gallinules creep along the edges of the marsh and Blue-grey Gnatcatchers flit in the trees above your head. As if this was not enough, large ponderous Alligators either swim silently by or lay motionless soaking up the sun.

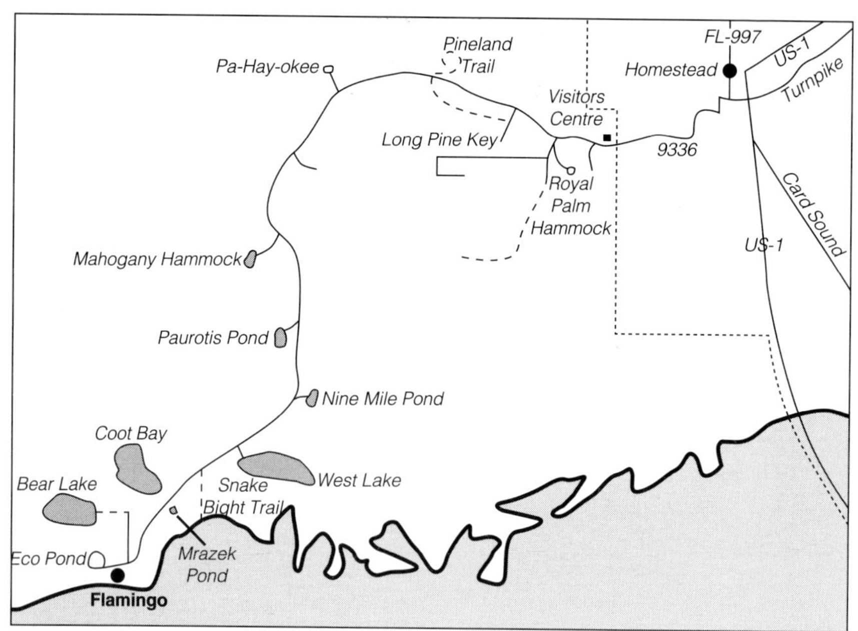

Site 6. Everglades National Park.

Heading back to the car you will have time for a stroll along The Gumbo Limbo Trail. This lush, almost tropical woodland is great for wintering warblers and with a little patience will come to view.

Driving on into the park there are many potential stopping places but many not so good for birds. The Pinelands Nature Trail is worth a stroll where, as you would expect, Pine Warbler is resident. This habitat is also good for Eastern Screech Owl and Barred Owl.

Mahogany Hammock is a key stop as this is one of the best places to get views of Barred Owl. Even in daylight with visitors around the birds will respond to vague imitations of their call.

Across from Mahogany Hammock there is a stand of pines which are frequently used by Bald Eagles for roosting and therefore are normally absent after the first hours of the day. Continuing on there are various ponds on either side of the road, but perhaps the most productive is Nine Mile Pond. Ospreys can be found fishing here as well as Caspian Terns and Forsters Terns.

Further towards Flamingo you will find the entry sign to the Snake Bight Trail. A bus with mosquito proof screens leaves from Flamingo and is recommended for the faint hearted. Otherwise slap on the repellant and dive in. The trail is nearly two miles long and goes through thick mangroves where, if you are lucky, a Mangrove Cuckoo may hurtle across the path. The author has never encountered so many mosquitoes and as he emerged frantically from the trailhead his wife remarked: "You looked as if you were on fire because the insects resembled smoke as they surrounded you". Do not give up because as you emerge onto the boardwalk overlooking Florida Bay you will see thousands of shorebirds and herons. These will include Reddish Egrets, White Pelicans, Great 'White' Herons, Western Sandpipers and Black Skimmers. What a sight! Now you only have to walk back again.

Now you will be at Flamingo where you could have booked ahead and stayed the night. You are confronted with a marina and a huge parking lot but watch out for flocks of Red-winged Blackbirds. Check the flocks for Brewers or Yellow-headed Blackbirds before looking into Florida Bay for more herons and shorebirds.

Move on to Eco Pond where you can stand on a tower to check out the birds. More egrets, herons and ibises and maybe a Mottled Duck. Look carefully because great rarities from the Caribbean have been found here. Search the scrub areas for Smooth-billed Anis.

Time your drive back for dusk and you should encounter Whip-poor-wills on the road and who knows maybe the very rare Puma will cross the road.

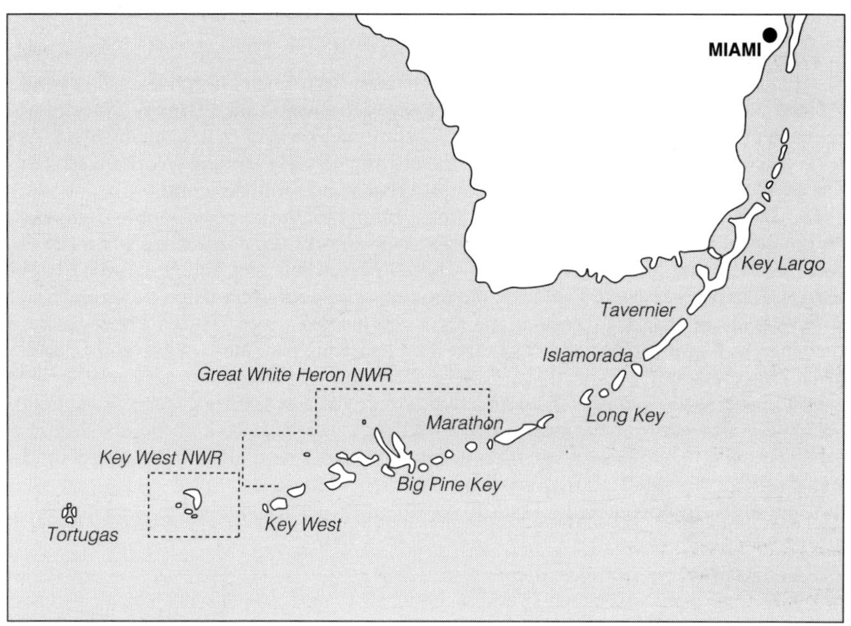

Site 7. Florida Keys.

7. The Keys

Many people say that the Keys are a waste of effort because they lack charm and are heavily urbanised. Well, that is true, but we all know now that birds are not necessarily bothered about aesthetics so give it a try. In a day from the Miami area you can cover a lot of ground if you start early and will probably reach Marathon before having to turn back.

Drive south on US-1 forking left for the Card Sound Road. Your first stop will probably be at Crocodile Lake where a few rare American Crocodiles are still to be found. Check shorebirds for Wilsons Plover. Head on checking any wooded area where in summer you should encounter Black-whiskered Vireo and White-crowned Pigeon. The author saw several of the latter fly across the road on a December drive.

A good place to halt is the Harry Harris County Park (Mile 93). Turn left into Burton Drive and follow signs to the Park. If there are not too many people you will get great views along the shore. Very tame Great 'White' Herons are here and Reddish Egret and many shorebirds. Ospreys fish offshore and Magnificent Frigate Birds cruise overhead. Check out the nearby church where there is a wet area amongst mangroves. This is a good spot for Roseate Spoonbills.

You can try the area around the Green Turtle Inn (Mile 81) which is said to be good for wintering Scissor-tailed Flycatcher and Western Kingbird. Smooth-billed Ani is also said to be in this region. Move on and check any of the many beaches for terns, gulls and shorebirds. Check carefully for Wilsons and Piping Plovers. Reddish Egrets and Brown Pelicans can be very approachable.

Try Lake Edna on Grassy Key by turning right on Peachtree Street (Mile 57.8). This lagoon has Reddish Egrets and American Avocets (winter) and sometimes Black-necked Stilts (summer).

At Marathon Key check out the airfield for Burrowing Owls and vagrant flycatchers on the wires.

If you want to carry on it is up to you but any further and you will need an overnight stop.

8. Shark Valley and the Tamiami Trail

The Tamiami Trail is in fact the US-41 running west from Miami to Naples and beyond.

Head out along the trail until you see the signs to Shark Valley. This is the northern entrance of The Everglades National Park. There is an excellent trail here which you can opt to walk, hire a cycle or take a ride on the environmentally friendly gas-powered tram. The cycle mode is best for covering the most ground and for finding birds.

The ditches have many Alligators and look carefully for the gorgeous Purple Gallinules. Multitudes of heron species, White Ibises and Wood Storks occur and when you reach the great tower search the bushes for Great Crested Flycatchers and Yellow-crowned Night Herons. Raptors are regular overhead, but look especially for Short-tailed Hawk and Snail Kite. White-tailed Deer are regular and Opossum has been seen. Skulking species are a challenge to find in the marshy edges but Sora and King Rail are possible and Limpkin much more obvious.

Head back to the Tamiami Trail and stop within yards at the Miccosukee Restaurant. Search the area north of the road for Snail Kites. These birds quarter the marshes in a manner similar to harriers and are most active in the early morning and late afternoon. In late afternoon thousands of Tree Swallows assemble to roost.

Keep on heading west to the Loop Road which eventually rejoins the Tamiami Trail. This is a good place to find Turkeys if you are here early.

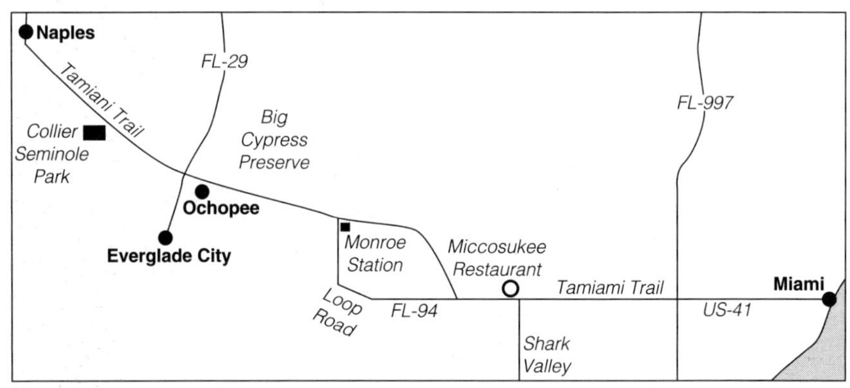

Site 8. Shark Valley and The Tamiami Trail.

9. Corkscrew Swamp

You can find this wonderful reserve via the SR-846 from Immokalee or Naples Park. The Corkscrew Swamp holds the largest stand of Bald Cypress left in Florida and as such is an outstanding habitat for wildlife. The main access is along a substantial boardwalk from which most of the birds can be seen.

In summer Swallow-tailed Kites, Yellow-throated Warblers and Pileated Woodpeckers nest. These giant trees also attract Wood Storks to breed in one of their largest nesting groups. Barred Owls are also resident and often seen at close quarters in broad daylight. Red-cockaded Woodpecker used to nest in the Slash Pine areas but is thought to have

Plate 19. *The typical Great Blue Heron also occurs in two rare plumage forms.*
David Hosking

Plate 20. *'Wurdemanns' Heron. A cross of the typical and white phases.*
David Hosking

Plate 21. *The Great 'White' Heron a white plumage form confined to South Florida.*
David Hosking

Plate 22. *You need to look carefully for the shy Yellow-crowned Night Heron.*
David Hosking

***Plate 23.** The Reddish Egret is not uncommon in coastal Florida.*

David Hosking

***Plate 24.** Look carefully in reedy places for the skulking Least Bittern.*

David Hosking

***Plate 25.** Sandhill Cranes can be found in urban areas as well as the more traditional wet grasslands.*

David Hosking

***Plate 26.** A Green Heron waits patiently for a passing morsel.*

Derek Moore

Plate 27. *Brown Pelicans are both obvious and spectacular around Florida's coast.*

David Hosking

Plate 28. *The strange Limpkin frequents dense marshes but can be quite confiding.*

Derek Moore

Plate 29. *Wood Storks are declining even in Florida.*

David Hosking

Plate 30. *Beaches can be crammed with birds just like these Laughing Gulls, Willets & Marbled Godwits.*

David Hosking

Plate 31. *Stunning rosy pink Roseate Spoonbills are best seen at the Ding Darling National Wildlife Refuge.*

David Hosking

disappeared from here now. Limpkins, Green-backed Herons and Anhingas make up the scene in this magical place.

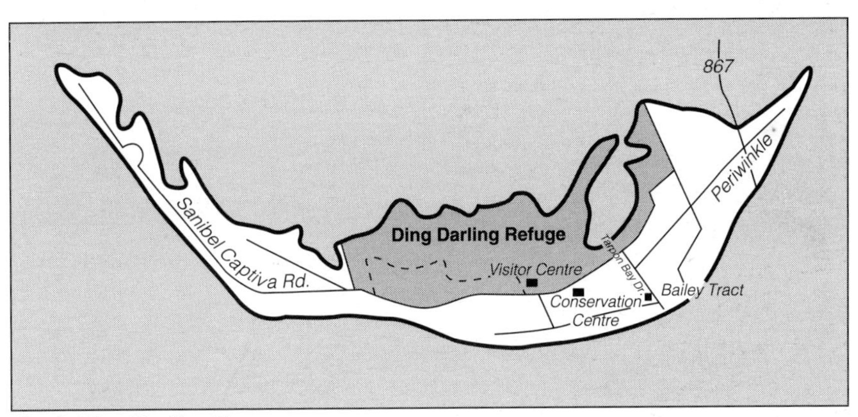

Site 9. Ding Darling Reserve.

10. Sanibel Island and Ding Darling National Wildlife Refuge

Situated on the west coast south-west of Fort Myers you have now strayed a fair way from Miami and indeed Orlando, but if you have to make one major trip to see some Florida birds then this has to be it.

You approach the causeway to the island on the SR-867 south of Fort Myers. Just before you reach the causeway there is a left turn down John Morris Road which is excellent for shorebirds if the tide is not too high. In winter large flocks of Least Sandpipers, Black-bellied Plovers, Sanderling, Red Knot, Short-billed Dowitchers, Western Sandpipers and Willets will be accompanied by smaller numbers of Wilsons Plovers, Marbled Godwits and American Oystercatchers. Forsters Terns and Black Skimmers fish nearby and maybe a Reddish Egret will put in an appearance. Bald Eagles and Ospreys patrol further out.

Head over the causeway looking out for more shorebirds and after reaching the island take a right on to Periwinkle Way and then a left into Tarpon Bay Road. You will find the Bailey Tract on the right. Here you can walk a series of dykes with various water bodies. Brown Pelicans and Magnificent Frigate Birds are often overhead and Least Bitterns skulk in the dense aquatic vegetation. Sadly Smooth-billed Anis have not been seen at this site for some time.

In summer Grey Kingbird, Swallow-tailed Kite, Black-winged Stilt, Mangrove Cuckoo and Black-whiskered Vireo all nest. Many migrants can be found here including vireos and warblers and occasionally Painted Bunting.

Retrace your way back along Tarpon Bay Road. Then join the Sanibel-Captiva Road until you see the signs for the Ding Darling National Wildlife Refuge. The reserve is open daily except Fridays. You can best enjoy this amazing place by leisurely driving the five-mile track. You should get out regularly to get to grips with the hordes of birds. Indeed, whenever birds occur you will almost certainly run into a major traffic jam and have to stop. If the tide is low you will see hundreds of herons, ibises, egrets and many Wood Storks and Roseate Spoonbills. Ospreys seem to be in flocks and Bald Eagles are present. In winter Peregrines hunt the numerous prey items. Peer once more into mangroves and exchange stares with Yellow-crowned Night Herons and motionless Anhingas. The open water will be full of Pied-billed Grebes, Blue-winged and Green-winged Teal in winter. Keep an eye overhead for Magnificent Frigate Birds and raptors such as Coopers Hawk and Red-shouldered Hawk. Hundreds of shorebirds include large numbers of Willets and both species of yellowlegs.

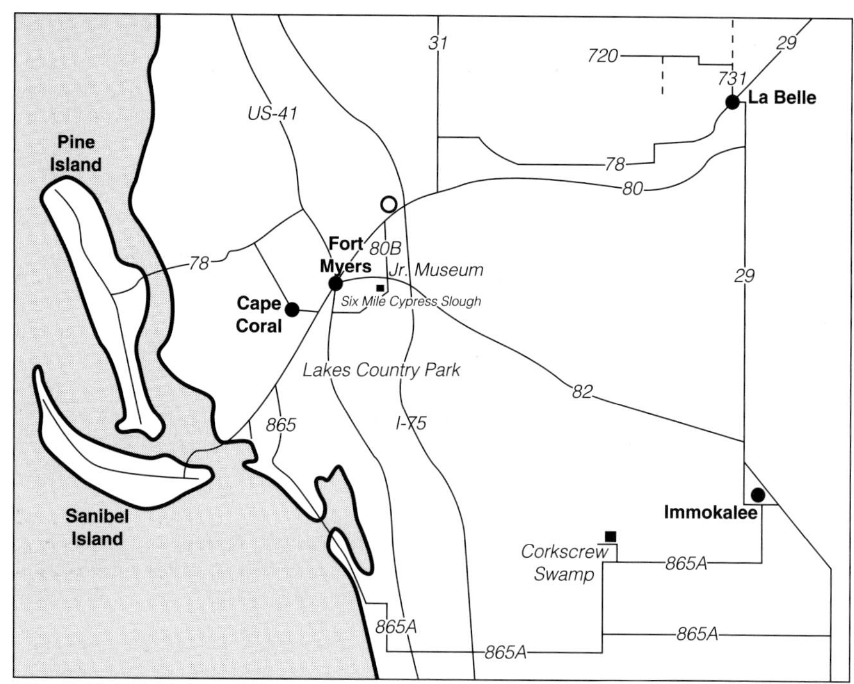

Sites 9,10,11&12. Fort Myers area.

An alternative for the energetic is to walk the South Dike Trail. Ospreys nest close to the route and excellent views can be obtained of herons and egrets. You can also walk the Shell Mound Trail where passerine migrants occur at peak times.

Finally, search amongst the numerous Alligators for American Crocodile as one has frequented the area in recent years. The American Crocodile is greenish rather than black and has a long tapered head with long snout. The Alligator's snout is very blunt. If the mouth is closed you can easily see the prominent teeth on the outside of the jaws.

11. Six Mile Cypress Slough Preserve

Head north on US-41 and then on the Six Mile Cypress Parkway. Turn right into Penzance Boulevard and then left into the parking area. The Preserve has over a mile of boardwalk trail through pond-cypress and mixed hardwood forest and a network of wetland habitats. A photo hide is available.

American Bittern, Wood Duck and Anhinga are usually present as well as other wetland species. Passage and wintering warblers can be found and check for River Otter which is very confiding here.

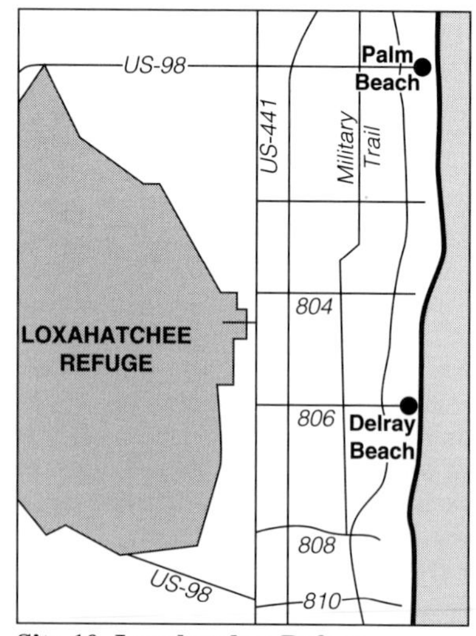

Site 10. Loxahatchee Refuge.

12. Lakes County Park

Take Summerlin Road east after leaving Sanibel Island and continue east on Gladiolus Drive where you will find the entrance on the left. A boardwalk and other trails traverse the woods, swamp and open water. A large heronry of mixed species can be viewed from the boardwalk.

13. Loxahatchee National Wildlife Refuge

Drive north of Miami on I-95 and leave at Exit 42 and then on SR-806 Atlantic Avenue until you meet US-441. Turn right and look out for the entrance on your left. Start your visit at the Visitor Centre and then consider taking both the main trails. The park is open daily in winter but only Wednesday through Sunday in summer.

The Cypress Walk is on a raised boardwalk and is good for Pileated Woodpecker and Barred Owl. The Marsh Trail is probably more productive as it encircles an impoundment of water. Here Fulvous Whistling Ducks and Mottled Ducks can be found in winter along with large numbers of Blue-winged and Green-winged Teal, American Wigeon, Lesser Scaup, Ring-necked Duck and Pintail. Check the bushes and scrub near this trail for Smooth-billed Ani.

You are welcome to walk the many other impoundments and in doing so you stand a good chance of seeing a Snail Kite. The birds are not always present but this is a very good site for this species. All around the Park you could see Limpkin, Purple Gallinule, Glossy Ibis, Wood Stork, Belted Kingfisher and many herons and egrets. Alligators are present in the open water areas.

Special Birds of the Sunshine State

Masked Booby *Sula dactylatra*
A few pairs breed annually on The Dry Tortugas. Otherwise a scarce visitor off both The Gulf and Atlantic coasts.

Brown Booby *Sula leucogaster*
Regular non-breeding resident of The Dry Tortugas. Regular off both coasts where it is often seen sitting on buoys and channel markers.

Magnificent Frigatebird *Fregata magnifiscens*
Most often found cruising the skies in coastal area. Sometimes the birds are extremely high so look up. Most often noted on The Keys, in Biscayne Bay and Sanibel Island.

American White Pelican *Pelecanus erythrorhynchos*
Mainly a winter visitor to Florida Bay, Biscayne Bay, Merritt Island and Sanibel Island. Occurring October to early May.

Brown Pelican *Pelecanus occidentalis*
Common in all coastal areas and very approachable. Not only do they perch on buoys, jetties and docks but also on roadside utility wires. How do they do that with those ungainly feet?

Anhinga *Anhinga anhinga*
Aptly called 'snake bird' by some. Most often seen sitting on trees or dyke banks with wings outstretched. Often soars when the 'cross-like' silhouette is unmistakable. Abundant throughout the state.

Great Blue Heron *Ardea herodias*
A common species throughout the United States but in Florida two interesting colour forms exist. The 'Great White' Heron occurs mostly in South Florida and is most often encountered south from Shark Valley and Miami and most common on The Keys. At first glance can be mistaken for Great Egret *(Ardea albus)* except for larger size and yellowish legs and feet. 'Wurdemmann's' Heron is a ghostly product of Great Blue and 'Great White' which has a white head and neck. Only found on the shores of Florida Bay.

Reddish Egret *Egretta rufescens*
An increasing species but still very uncommon. Found at Merritt Island, Sanibel Island, Flamingo, the end of the Snake Bight Trail and The Keys. Feeds by dancing with wings outstretched. A rare white form is sometimes seen.

White Ibis *Eudocimus albus*
Very common throughout the state. Most often found in flocks which often contain immature birds which are dull brown. Watch out for their 'V' formation roosting flights.

Roseate Spoonbill *Ajaia ajaja*
Not uncommon. Prefers estuarine habitats with mangrove swamps. Unmistakable birds especially when in the full pink flush of breeding plumage. Seen at Merritt Island, The Everglades and best of all at Sanibel Island.

Greater Flamingo *Phoenicopterus ruber*
Birds do occur in the extreme south-west particularly in winter. Some feral birds probably exist in the area but genuine vagrants from The Caribbean are possible.

Wood Stork *Mycteria americana*
Still numerous even though the population is declining. Found throughout the area, particularly in The Corkscrew Swamp where a large colony nests.

Fulvous Whistling Duck *Dendrocygna bicolor*
A resident of the region which occasionally occurs in large flocks. Several thousand are found in winter at Loxahatchee.

Black-bellied Whistling Duck *Dendrocygna autumnalis*
An increasing species of the central part of Florida and in particular the district just to the south-east of Sarasota. The population is very local but this species should be looked for wherever wildfowl gather.

Mottled Duck *Anas fulvigula*
Most often seen at Merritt Island, Lake Okeechobee and Loxahatchee.

Osprey *Pandion haliaetus*
Very common wherever there is water. Nests in some very accessible places including utility poles on the central reservations of highways. Sanibel Island, The Everglades and Merritt Island are favoured haunts.

Swallow-tailed Kite *Elanoides forficatus*
Fairly common nesting visitor from February to September. Breeds in most habitats with trees, building a nest of Spanish Moss.

Snail Kite *Rostrhamus sociabilis*
Confined to Florida in the USA and most likely to be seen at Loxahatchee and along the Tamiami Trail. also seen near Clewiston on the south shore of Lake Okeechobee. As its name implies, this bird feeds exclusively on snails so the habitat frequented tends to be very specific. Most obvious in early mornings and evenings when the prey becomes most active.

Bald Eagle *Haliseetus leucocephalus*
A stable population exists throughout the area. Good concentrations can be found in The Everglades and the Lake Kissimmee State Park.

Red-shouldered Hawk *Buteo lineatus*
The striking pale and small Florida race occurs almost everywhere.

Short-tailed Hawk *Buteo brachyurus*
Uncommon. Dark and pale colour phases occur and this species nests throughout Florida. There is a noticeable migration to the southern part of the state in winter.

Crested Caracara *Polyborus planeus*
Uncommon resident of the grassy prairies north and west of Lake Okeechobee. Particularly likes sitting on the tops of Cabbage Palms. Feeds on carrion and often flushed from road kills.

Black Rail *Laterallus jamaicensis*
An extremely secretive and somewhat mystical species. Probably quite rare in dense marshes. Lake Woodruff National Wildlife Refuge is said to be a good site for this species as is the area around Titsville. The St. John's National Wildlife Refuge is another good site.

Purple Gallinule *Porphyrula martinica*
A brilliantly coloured resident of marshes and bogs. Some very tame individuals occur in The Everglades especially at Royal Palm.

Limpkin *Aramus guarauna*
Although often nocturnal this species can be seen in daylight particularly if cloudy. Utters a frightening loud mournful cry. Loxahatchee, Lake Woodruff National Wildlife Refuge and The Prairie Lakes Reserve are a good bet. Eats snails so frequents similar areas to Snail Kite.

Sandhill Crane *Grus canadensis*
The race found in Florida is non-migratory and found throughout the area. Although present in The Everglades it is more common in the Orlando region.

Whooping Crane *Grus americana*
Since 1993 this species has been reintroduced into The Three Lakes Wildlife Management Area to the south-east of Orlando. You should watch out for this species anywhere around Lake Kissimmee and of course the Three Lakes area.

Wilson's Plover *Charadrius wilsonia*
A very local resident of Gulf Coast beaches. Look for this bird on Bunche Beach at the end of John Morris Road. You find this spot just before the bridge to Sanibel Island after taking a left off MacGregor Boulevard.

Piping Plover *Charadrius melodus*
An uncommon winter visitor of sandy beaches. Mainly found on the Gulf Coast but also encountered on The Keys. A very small pale plover which runs fast like a tiny clockwork toy.

American Oystercatcher *Haematopus palliatus*
An uncommon coastal resident mainly found on the Gulf Coast and The Keys. Fort Myers beach is a favoured locality.

Black-necked Stilt *Himantopus mexicanus*
Often encountered in spring and summer. Zellwood is a very favoured site and it can also be found on Merritt Island in the nesting season. Occasionally noted in winter.

American Avocet *Recurvirostra americana*
Local winter visitor with sizeable flocks at Merritt Island, Mckay Bay and at impoundments in Polk County.

Long-billed Curlew *Numenius americanus*
Rare but pretty regular winter resident. The Gulf Coast is favoured and Fort Myers beach is the best bet.

Marbled Godwit *Limosa fedoa*
Another winter visitor which favours the Gulf Coast. Usually encountered at Bunche Beach, Fort Myers Beach and in Flamingo Bay. Also present on Merritt Island.

Bridled Tern *Sterna anaethetus*
A few pairs breed off Key West; otherwise an offshore visitor to the south-east coast and The Keys.

Sooty Tern *Sterna fuscata*
Up to 40,000 pairs breed on The Dry Tortugas. Elsewhere a very rare visitor during the summer months.

Brown Noddy *Anous stolidus*
Also a rare coastal visitor except for about 2,000 pairs nesting on Bush Key in The Dry Tortugas.

Black Skimmer *Rynchops niger*
A common bird of coastal areas. Check out parking lots and jetties as well as beach areas.

White-crowned Pigeon *Columba leucocephala*
The white crown is sometimes difficult to see in the field so look hard at any black pigeons. Summers in mangroves and hardwoods in the southern Everglades, Sanibel Island and The Keys. A few winter and seem regular at Matheson Hammock.

White-winged Dove *Zenaida asiatica*
An introduced species of urban areas. Castello Hammock in Homestead is a good place to see this species.

Common Ground Dove *Columbina passerina*
Very common. An extremely small dove which feeds on short grassy areas. Prefers to run into cover rather than fly.

Monk Parakeet *Myiopsitia monachus*
An introduced species which has established viable populations in urban areas. Most numerous in the Tampa Bay district and from Fort Lauderdale to Miami.

Canary-winged Parakeet *Brotogeris versicolorus*
Once very numerous in south Miami where large flocks could be seen and heard going to roost. One of the commonest of the parrot species which escaped and formed thriving feral colonies but now declining.

Mangrove Cuckoo *Coccyzus minor*
Uncommon summer visitor to mangrove forests. Very secretive in habits. Good sites are Snake Bight Trail, Biscayne Bay and Sanibel Island.

Smooth-billed Ani *Crotophaga ani*
Often secretive and skulking. Loves scrubby areas near agricultural fields, thickets and even urban sites. Look for this strange species at Loxahatchee and Eco Pond near Flamingo.

Burrowing Owl *Athene cunicularia*
A resident of sandy, flat areas such as golf courses and airstrips. Can be quite numerous and colonial in some places. Homestead airfield and Cape Coral are very good sites for this species.

Barred Owl *Strix varia*
An often obvious resident of Cypress stands and hammock woodlands. Mahogany Hammock in The Everglades National Park is a well known site for this bird.

Antillean Nighthawk *Chordeiles gundlachii*
Summer resident of The Keys and probably the Homestead area. Voice a distinctive *pity-pit-pit* or *killy-kadick.*

Chuck-will's-widow *Caprimulgus carolinensis*
Summer resident with some wintering in the south. Try driving roads at night for views of this crepuscular creature. More often heard than seen. Calls its name.

Ruby-throated Hummingbird *Archilochus colubris*
Uncommon resident and winter visitor in the south. Fairchild Gardens is a good site to find these little gems in winter.

Red-headed Woodpecker *Melanerpes erythrocephalus*
Prefers sandy areas with scattered pine woodland. Lake Kissimmee State Park is a good place for this bird.

Red-cockaded Woodpecker *Picoides borealis*
A rare resident of the extensive pines woodlands. Long-leaved Pine seems to be a prime requirement of this bird. They seem to move around in small flocks quite a lot but they are elusive and you need to check for recent sightings. The Ocala Forest is an excellent location for this species.

Western Kingbird *Tyrannus verticalis*
A scarce winter visitor to the extreme south. Look for this bird on The Keys and from Homestead south.

Grey Kingbird *Tyrannus dominicensis*
A common summer resident frequenting mangroves and other scrubby areas close to water.

Scissor-tailed Flycatcher *Muscivora forficata*
Migrants occur on the Gulf Coast but in winter this species can be found on The Keys. Look on the utility lines; you cannot miss an adult with its long tail streamers.

Florida Scrub Jay *Aphelocoma coerulscens*
Recently split from two similar species in California. This attractive bird can be found all year near Lake Placid, Lake Kissimmee State Park and the Ocala Forest.

Cave Swallow *Hirundo fulva*
Since 1987 a small colony has been discovered nesting on bridges in the Homestead area. Only present January until late September.

Brown-headed Nuthatch *Sitta pusilla*
A rare resident of mature pine woodlands. Lake Kissimmee State Park is a good area.

Red-whiskered Bulbul *Pycnonotus jocosus*
Introduced and established in the district of Kendall in Miami. The Kendall tennis courts are a favoured area.

Black-whiskered Vireo *Vireo altiloquus*
A common summer visitor to mangroves and hammocks.

Yellow Warbler *Dendroica petechia*
A common migrant but watch out for the race *Dendroica petechia gundlachi* often referred to as Cuban Yellow Warbler. This form occurs in the mangroves of the south-west and The Keys. The races cannot be split on plumage only on breeding range.

Yellow-throated Warbler *Dendroica dominica*
Nests locally in The Panhandle and north and winters south to The Keys. Check out the warbler flocks for this striking bird.

Pine Warbler *Dendroica pinus*
A common all year resident of pine woodlands.

Prairie Warbler *Dendroica discolor*
Uncommon resident and passage migrant. The resident population nests in mangroves in the south.

Prothonotary Warbler *Prothonotaria citrea*
The first problem is to learn how to pronounce the name of this bird. Breeds commonly in wetlands in the northern part of the state.

Summer Tanager *Piranga rubra*
Reasonably common breeding bird of hammocks, pinelands and sandy areas. Not found nesting in the south.

Painted Bunting *Passerina ciris*
The male is a truly gorgeous creature which together with the drabber green females frequents feeders in winter. Castello Hammock is a well known spot for this bird. A resident species.

Plate 32. *The skulking Sora Rail inhabits dense aquatic vegetation.*

David Hosking

Plate 33. *Royal Terns are common and often rest on secluded beaches.*

David Hosking

Plate 34. *Black Skimmers fish by scooping up prey with the elongated lower mandible.*

David Hosking

Plate 35. *The Anhinga or Snake Bird is a close relative of cormorants.*

David Hosking

Plate 36. *The brightly coloured Purple Gallinule is often very approachable.*

David Hosking

Plate 37. *Burrowing Owls are most endearing and very tame.*

David Hosking

Plate 38. *Adult Little Blue Heron, a widespread species.*

David Hosking

Plate 39. *Juvenile Little Blue Heron; sometimes confused with Snowy Egret.*

David Hosking

Plate 40. *The Red-bellied Woodpecker is found in most wooded habitats.*

David Hosking

Plate 41. *The spectacular Painted Bunting often visits feeders in winter.*

Derek Moore

Plate 42. *Palm Warbler is one of the most common warblers to be found in winter.*

David Hosking

Plate 43. *The smooth-billed Ani can be very elusive.*

David Hosking

Plate 44. *The typical 'smile' of the rare American Crocodile.*

David Hosking

Plate 45. *Alligators are very common in Florida.*

David Hosking

Plate 46. *Comical Armadillos can be encountered in areas with light sandy soil.*

David Hosking

Plate 47. *The ponderous Manatee often frequents the permanently warm waters near power stations in winter.*

Derek Moore

Bachman's Sparrow *Aimophila aestivalis*
An uncommon resident of pine woodland with Palmetto Palms. Very secretive and skulking. Lake Kissimmee State Park and Ocala Forest are good places.

Seaside Sparrow *Ammodramus maritimus*
The distinct Cape Sable race occurs in the Cape Sable marshes and at Taylor Slough in The Everglades. This bird is very secretive and you will have to be very patient to see one. Another distinct race, the Dusky Seaside Sparrow, which was found on the upper St John's River and Merritt Isdland, is now considered extinct.

Spot-breasted Oriole *Icterus pectoralis*
Probably introduced and confined to urban areas in the Miami region. Look for them feeding on nectar wherever there are flowering trees and shrubs. Fairchild Gardens is a good site.

Exotic Escapes
Almost anything is possible in Florida, particularly in the Miami area, where many parrots and other tropical species have escaped and in some cases formed viable populations. Keep an open mind and do not be surprised at what you might find.

Getting the best from your Camera by David Hosking

There is no substitute for proper preparation for any birding trip, whether you're planning to stay at home or go abroad, taking a camera and lenses with you to photograph birds adds a whole new dimension to the planning stage. There are certain things that should be done to make life that bit easier before you start and good planning will let you make the most of your trip.

One unbreakable rule is never to take along untried or untested equipment. If you buy new equipment for use on a trip make sure you familiarise yourself with its characteristics before departure. This applies equally to cameras, lenses, binoculars and even new types of film: use the equipment as much and in as wide a range of conditions as possible, making notes so that the results can be easily assessed. Only when the new equipment produces satisfactory photographs and you are fully conversant with its operation should it be added to your packing list. It's a very good idea to keep a packing list as it is so easy to forget a vital accessory.

Another important pre-travel chore is to confirm that your camera equipment is adequately insured. Most travel insurance policies do not cover photographic equipment worth more an a few hundred pounds. Some other policies may not cover North America. A list of all your equipment serial numbers, supported by photocopies of receipts, can be helpful at airports and customs, particularly if equipment is new looking.

So what should you take? Here are some suggestions:

Cameras

The interchangeable lens facility and unrivalled flexibility of a 35mm single lens reflex (SLR) camera makes this the obvious choice for most bird photographers. Auto focus is a standard built in feature of most 35mm cameras and is an invaluable aid to taking top quality photographs. In some travel locations where animals are more approachable, medium format cameras that use 120 film are also suitable. As usual though there is a trade off and the merit of the medium format's larger image must be set against the greater weight of the equipment and its slower speed of use.

A reliable back-up camera is a virtual necessity as an insurance against camera malfunction when you're away. The extra expense is a small price to pay for peace of mind. Two identical SLR's are ideal but if this is not feasible, choose a back-up model that is at least lens compatible with your main camera.

Many of today's cameras and binoculars are quite heavy. A wide camera strap distributes the burden and can greatly reduce the discomfort on long travels. Some types even have a degree of elasticity, which further reduces the strain.

It is good practice to check and clean your camera and optical equipment each night before turning in. Dust is a perennial enemy and a single speck on the film pressure plate can ruin all your film. A rubber blower brush is useful for keeping the camera back dust-free. Lenses should obviously be kept clean at all times as even a small amount of dirt will cause flare and a general loss of picture quality.

Lenses and Filters

Zoom lenses are favoured by many photographers because they give precise control over picture composition. A complete range of focal lengths can be provided by just two zooms, such as a 28-80mm which is great for recording habitats and an 70-300mm, which will be the most useful lens for recording wildlife. Lastly for the more adventurous a fixed focal length of 400mm or 500mm is desirable for taking bird portraits. These fixed focal length lenses can be increased by using a teleconverter which fits between the camera and the lens. A x1.4 teleconverter increases a 400mm lens to 560mm. This increase in magnification brings with it a marked reduction in speed by reducing the maximum aperture by one full f-stop with a x1.4 and two stops with a x2 teleconverter.

All lenses should be protected from dust rain, finger marks and scratches by fitting a filter. An ultra violet (UV) filter is best as it reduces haze but does not affect colour temperature or exposure. Make sure that the optical quality of the filter you fit is at least as good as that of your lens, fitting a cheap uncoated filter to an expensive lens will unnecessarily diminish the quality of your photographs. Under certain light conditions a Polarizing filter can be used to deepen sky colouration, increase contrast and reduce reflections.

Film

Whether to use slide or print film depends on your requirements, prints are easier to view but slides are more versatile. Which ever you decide on, the superb sharpness exhibited by fine grain films of ISO 50 or 100 makes them well worth consideration. How much film should you take? Go through your itinerary and estimate your daily film requirements, calculate the total and then double it! While most types and makes of film are available in Florida it will save time to always have plenty with you.

Most major international airports should by now employ security scanning equipment that should not harm your film. It is most unlikely that two or three passes through an X-ray machine will do any damage. Slower film is less sensitive to X-rays. Lead bags could be used but usually attracts attention and are heavy. If you are worried about having your film X rayed, then ask for a hand search which might be possible. To make hand searches at busy air ports quicker remove films from their boxes (but not their canisters these are waterproof). If you have more than one film type, make sure each is recognisable by labelling the canisters with a permanent marker. Some canisters such as Fuji are transparent and greatly facilitating airport checks.

The boxes that some slides are returned from processing in are excellent way of carrying film: four films fit into a box and a number of boxes are easier to pack than many rolls of loose film. Security officers may occasionally wish to open a camera back, so it is sensible to carry cameras empty of film.

Take care to change films in the shade – even if your body is the only source remember the Florida sunlight is particularly intense. By fully rewinding films into their cassettes there is no possibility of reloading an exposed film. Avoid placing your equipment next to air conditioners, as they can cause condensation problems by rapid temperature changes.

Keeping a daily record of all the places visited and subjects photographed is essential. Memories are notoriously unreliable and to be able to confidently and accurately label your photographs, you must have dependable notes. It can help to label each used film canister with a consecutive number and the date, so you can match each day's photography to your diary. An electronic notebook is a popular way of keeping notes while out in the field.

Camera Bags

Having invested in a good camera system it does not make sense to skimp on a camera bag. Overseas travel often entails more demanding transport and climatic conditions than at home. Inevitably your camera equipment is prone to certain amount of mistreatment and must be effectively safe guarded against damage.

There are many well designed bags to choose from and the best offer ample protection from shocks, as well as being waterproof. Study the alternatives before making your final choice and take your camera gear along to be certain that the bag is sufficiently large, not too heavy and gives easy access.

Avoid the temptation to get a bag that to too big: carrying an overladen camera bag is a recipe for poor photography, as you quickly tire and lose the edge to your concentration. Another consideration is the size restrictions imposed by airlines on cabin luggage. As well as a shoulder strap, some camera bags come with a rucksack frame, which are much more comfortable for carrying equipment in the field.

Any cosmetic camouflaging that can be applied to camera bags to make them appear less obvious is a useful security precaution. It is a good idea to keep a few bags of silica gel in your camera bag to absorb any dampness. From time to time the gel can be reactivated by heating it for a few minutes in a warm oven.

Camera Supports

As the commonest cause of picture failure is camera shake, the use of a support, such as a tripod is critical and a must when using the 400mm and 500mm lenses. While weight is probably the single most restrictive factor to bear in mind when assembling your equipment for a trip, a tripod must be sturdy and therefore heavy.

Monopods present a lightweight and easier to use alternative and, with practice can be used to hold even long telephoto steady. Beanbags are also very effective when used in conjunction with a tree, rock or car window frame.

Other accessories

Spare batteries are essential for all items of photographic equipment, including cameras, motordrives, flashguns, torches and electronic note books. Double check your instruction manual to ensure you stock up with the correct types. Putting fresh batteries in your camera before you leave home makes sense – battery failure always strikes just as the action starts! Remember that auto focus cameras have prodigious power requirements and, consequently, demand plenty of spare batteries.

It is also worth noting that rechargeable batteries lose their charge more quickly than ordinary ones, but are less affected by low temperature than disposable batteries.

A supply of small and large plastic bags always comes in handy for keeping dust and water, especially seawater away from camera equipment.

General Notes

Florida is one of the best places in the world to photograph wildlife. The tameness of the many species, particularly the egrets and herons, offer a wealth of opportunity to take successful and rewarding pictures. Remember there is much more to bird photography than pointing and shooting your camera. A good picture is made by its composition so a few points to remember:

- Does this look best as a landscape or vertical shape.
- Be sure to keep the horizon level.
- How big do I want the bird in my picture.
- Have I got a catch light in the birds eyes.
- Is the bird looking into or out of my picture.
- Pay particular attention to the background to ensure it is free of distracting elements.
- Do not be afraid to get down low as this can often produce dramatic results.
- Light is the key element in any photograph so be alert to new possibilities as it changes.

Wildlife photography can bring a tremendous amount of pleasure and satisfaction but remember the subject is always more important than your picture.

Do not neglect to take photographs to show where you travelled, novel modes of transport and lodgings and so on. In other words aim to capture the whole story of your trip on film, if you are planning to produce a slide talk after your trip, it will be much more interesting for your audience, if you put your bird photographs into context. A compact camera is the ideal way of recording this sort of information.

And last, but not least have a good trip.

Checklist of the Birds of Florida

Introduced species which have established sustainable feral populations have been included. Also included are species found on the Dry Tortugas situated off The Keys, even though these are unlikely to be encountered without a visit to these remote islands.

Key to symbols:

RB — Resident Breeder MB — Migrant Breeder OB — Occasional Breeder

PM — Passage Migrant WV — Winter Visitor AV — Accidental Visitor

* Introduced species and now breeding in a sustainable feral state.

English name	Scientific name	Status
Red-throated Loon	*Gavia stellata*	WV
Common Loon	*Gavia immer*	WV
Pied-billed Grebe	*Podilymbus podiceps*	WV RB
Horned Grebe	*Podiceps auritus*	WV
Black-capped Petrel (Atlantic only)	*Pterodroma hasitata*	PM
Cory's Shearwater	*Calonectris diomedea*	PM
Great Shearwater	*Puffinis gravis*	PM
Audubon's Shearwater	*Puffinis iherminieri*	PM
Wilson's Petrel	*Oceanites oceanicus*	PM
Leach's Petrel	*Oceanodroma leucohoa*	AV
White-tailed Tropic Bird (Tortugas)	*Phaethon lepturus*	AV
Masked Booby (Tortugas)	*Sula dactylatra*	RB
Brown Booby (Tortugas)	*Sula leucogaster*	RB
Red-footed Booby (Tortugas)	*SDula sula*	AV
Northern Gannet	*Sula bassanus*	WV
American White Pelican	*Pelecanus erythrorhynchos*	WV
Brown Pelican	*Pelecanus occidentalis*	RB
Great Cormorant	*Phalacrocorax carbo*	WV
Double-crested Cormorant	*Phalacrocorax auritus*	RB
Anhinga	*Anhinga anhinga*	RB
Magnificent Frigatebird	*Fregata magnificens*	RB
American Bittern	*Botaurus lentiginosus*	WV
Least Bittern	*Ixobrychus exilis*	RB
Great Blue Heron	*Ardea herodias*	RB
Great Egret	*Ardea albus*	RB
Snowy Egret	*Egretta thula*	RB
Little Blue Heron	*Egretta caerulea*	RB
Tri-coloured Heron	*Egretta tricolor*	RB
Reddish Egret	*Egretta rufescens*	RB
Cattle Egret	*Bubulcus ibis*	RB
Green Heron	*Butorides striatus*	RB
Black-crowned Night Heron	*Nycticorax nycticorax*	RB
Yellow-crowned Night Heron	*Nycticorax violaceus*	RB
White Ibis	*Eudocimus albus*	RB
Glossy Ibis	*Plegadis falcinellus*	RB
Roseate Spoonbill	*Ajaia ajaja*	RB
Wood Stork	*Mycteria americana*	RB
Greater Flamingo	*Phoenicopterus ruber*	AV
Fulvous Whistling Duck	*Dendrocygna bicolor*	RB
Black-bellied Whistling Duck	*Dendrocygna autumnalis*	RB

English name	Scientific name	Status
Snow Goose	*Chen caerulescens*	WV
Brant	*Branta bernicla*	WV
Canada Goose	*Branta canadensis*	WV
Wood Duck	*Aix sponsa*	RB
Green-winged Teal	*Anas crecca*	WV
American Black Duck	*Anas rubripes*	WV
Mottled Duck	*Anas fulvigula*	RB
Mallard	*Anas platyrhynchos*	WV
Northern Pintail	*Anas acuta*	WV
Blue-winged Teal	*Anas discors*	WV
Cinnamon Teal	*Anas cyanoptera*	AV
Northern Shoveler	*Anas clypeata*	WV
Gadwall	*Anas strepera*	WV
Eurasian Wigeon	*Anas penelope*	AV
American Wigeon	*Anas americana*	WV
Canvasback	*Aythya valisineria*	WV
Redhead	*Aythya americana*	WV
Ring-necked Duck	*Aythya collaris*	WV
Greater Scaup	*Aythya marila*	WV
Lesser Scaup	*Aythya affinis*	WV
Oldsquaw	*Clangula hyemalis*	WV
Black Scoter	*Melanitta nigra*	WV
Surf Scoter	*Melanitta perspicillata*	WV
White-winged Scoter	*Melanitta fusca*	AV
Goldeneye	*Bucephala clangula*	WV
Bufflehead	*Bucephala albeola*	WV
Hooded Merganser	*Lophodytes cucullatus*	WV
Common Merganser	*Mergus merganser*	WV
Red-breasted Merganser	*Mergus serrator*	WV
Ruddy Duck	*Oxyura jamaicensis*	WV
Masked Duck	*Oxyura dominica*	AV
Black Vulture	*Coragyps atratus*	RB
Turkey Vulture	*Cathartes aura*	RB
Osprey	*Pandion haliaetus*	RB
Swallow-tailed Kite	*Elanoides forficatus*	MB
White-tailed Kite	*Elanus leucurus*	RB
Snail Kite	*Rostrhamus sociabilis*	RB
Mississippi Kite	*Ictinia mississippiensis*	MB
Bald Eagle	*Haliaeetus leucocephalus*	RB
Northern Harrier	*Circus cyaneus*	WV
Sharp-shinned Hawk	*Accipiter striatus*	WV
Coopers Hawk	*Accipiter cooperii*	WV
Common Black Hawk	*Buteogallus anthracinus*	AV
Red-shouldered Hawk	*Buteo lineatus*	RB
Broad-winged Hawk	*Buteo platypterus*	RB WV
Swainson's Hawk	*Buteo swainsoni*	WV
Short-tailed Hawk	*Buteo brachyurus*	RB
Red-tailed Hawk	*Buteo Jamaicensis*	RB
Rough-legged Hawk	*Buteo lagopus*	AV
Golden Eagle	*Aquila chrysaetos*	WV
Crested Caracara	*Polyborus planeus*	RB

English name	Scientific name	Status
American Kestrel	*Falco sparverius*	RB WV
Merlin	*Falco columbarius*	WV
Peregrine	*Falco peregrinus*	WV
Wild Turkey	*Meleagris gallopavo*	RB
Northern Bobwhite	*Colinus virginianus*	RB
Yellow Rail	*Cturnicops noveboracensis*	WV
Black Rail	*Laterallus jamaicensis*	RB WV
Clapper Rail	*Rallus longirostris*	RB
King Rail	*Rallus elegans*	RB
Virginia Rail	*Rallus limicola*	WV
Sora	*Porzana carolina*	WV
Purple Gallinule	*Porphrula martinica*	RB
Moorhen	*Gallinula chloropus*	RB
American Coot	*Fulica americana*	RB
Caribbean Coot	*Fulica caribaes*	AV
Limpkin	*Aramus guarauna*	RB
Sandhill Crane	*Grus canadensis*	RB
Whooping Crane*	*Grus americana*	RB
Black-bellied Plover	*Pluvialis squatarola*	WV
American Golden Plover	*Pluvialis dominica*	PM
Snowy Plover (Gulf Coast only)	*Charadrius alexandrinus*	RB
Wilson's Plover	*Charadrius wilsonia*	RB
Semi-palmated Plover	*Charadrius semipalmatus*	WV PM
Piping Plover	*Charadrius melodus*	WV
Killdeer	*Charadrius vociferus*	RB PM
American Oystercatcher	*Haematopus palliatus*	RB
Black-necked Stilt	*Himantopus mexicanus*	MB WV
American Avocet	*Recurvirostra americana*	WV PM
Greater Yellowlegs	*Tringa melanoleuca*	WV PM
Lesser Yellowlegs	*Tringa flavipes*	WV PM
Solitary Sandpiper	*Tringa solitaria*	PM
Willet	*Catoptrophorus semipalmatus*	RB
Spotted Sandpiper	*Actitis macularia*	WV PM
Upland Sandpiper	*Bartramia longicauda*	PM
Whimbrel	*Numenius phaeopus*	PM
Long-billed Curlew	*Numenius americanus*	AV
Marbled Godwit	*Limosa fedoa*	WV
Ruddy Turnstone	*Arenaria interpres*	WV
Red Knot	*Calidris canutus*	PM
Sanderling	*Calidris alba*	WV
Semipalmated Sandpiper	*Calidris pusilla*	PM
Western Sandpiper	*Calidris mauri*	WV
Least Sandpiper	*Calidris minutilla*	WV
White-rumped Sandpiper	*Calidris fuscicollis*	PM
Baird's Sandpiper	*Calidris bairdii*	AV
Pectoral Sandpiper	*Calidris melanotos*	PM
Purple Sandpiper	*Calidris maritima*	AV
Dunlin	*Calidris alpina*	WV
Stilt Sandpiper	*Calidris himantopus*	PM
Buff-breasted Sandpiper	*Tryngites subruficollis*	AV
Ruff	*Philomachus pugnax*	AV

English name	Scientific name	Status
Short-billed Dowitcher	*Limnodromus griseus*	WV PM
Long-billed Dowitcher	*Limnodromuis scolopaceus*	WV PM
Common Snipe	*Gallinago gallinago*	WV
American Woodcock	*Scolopax minor*	WV PM
Wilson's Phalarope	*Phalaropus tricolor*	PM
Red-necked Phalarope (Atlantic only)	*Phalaropus lobatus*	PM
Red Phalarope (Atlantic only)	*Phalaropus fulicaria*	WV PM
Pomarine Jaeger	*Stercorarius pomarinus*	WV PM
Parasitic Jaeger	*Stercorarius parasiticus*	WV PM
Laughing Gull	*Larus atricilla*	RB
Bonaparte's Gull	*Larus philadelphia*	WV
Ring-billed Gull	*Larus delawarensis*	WV
Herring Gull	*Larus argentatus*	WV
Iceland Gull	*Larus glaucoides*	AV
Lesser black-backed Gull	*Larus fuscus*	WV
Great Black-backed Gull	*Larus marinus*	WV
Black-legged Kittiwake	*Rissa trydactyla*	WV
Gull-billed Tern	*Sterna nilotica*	RB
Caspian Tern	*Sterna caspia*	RB
Royal Tern	*Sterna maxima*	RB
Sandwich Tern	*Sterna sandvicensis*	RB
Roseate Tern	*Sterna dougallii*	MB
Common Tern	*Sterna hirundo*	WV
Forster's Tern	*Sterna forsteri*	WV PM
Least Tern	*Sterna antillarum*	MB
Bridled Tern	*Sterna anaethetus*	AV
Sooty Tern (mainly Tortugas)	*Sterna fuscata*	MB
Black Tern	*Chlidonias niger*	PM
Brown Noddy (mainly Tortugas)	*Anous stolidus*	MB
Black Noddy (mainly Tortugas)	*Anous minutus*	AV
Black Skimmer	*Rynchops niger*	RB
Rock Dove	*Columba livia*	RB
White-crowned Pigeon	*Columba leucocephala*	MB WV
Eurasian Collared Dove*	*Streptopelia decaocto*	RB
White-winged Dove*	*Zenaida asiatica*	RB
Mourning Dove	*Zenaida macroura*	RB
Common Ground Dove	*Colubina passerina*	RB
Budgerigar (Gulf coast)*	*Melopsittacus undulatus*	RB
Rose-ringed Parakeet (Dade County)*	*Psitticula krameri*	RB
Monk Parakeet*	*Myiopsitta monachus*	RB
Canary-winged Parakeet (Miami area)*	*Brotogeris versicolorus*	RB
Red-crowned Parrot (Miami area)*	*Amazona viridigenalis*	RB
Black-billed Cuckoo	*Coccyzus erythropthalmus*	PM
Yellow-billed Cuckoo	*Coccyzus americanus*	MB PM
Mangrove Cuckoo	*Coccyzus minor*	MB
Smooth-billed Ani	*Crotophaga ani*	RB
Groove-billed Ani	*Crotophaga sulcirostris*	AV
Barn Owl	*Tyto alba*	RB
Eastern Screech Owl	*Otus asio*	RB
Great Horned Owl	*Bubo virginianus*	RB
Burrowing Owl	*Athene cunicularia*	RB

English name	Scientific name	Status
Barred Owl	*Strix varia*	RB
Short-eared Owl	*Asio flammeus*	WV
Common Nighthawk	*Chordeiles minor*	MB PM
Antillean Nighthawk	*Chordeiles gundlachii*	MB
Chuck-will's-widow	*Caprimulgus carolinensis*	MB WV
Whip-poor-will	*Caprimulgus vociferus*	WV
Chimney Swift	*Chaetura pelagica*	MB
Ruby-throated Hummingbird	*Archilochus colubris*	RB WV
Rufous Hummingbird	*Selasphorus rufus*	AV
Belted Kingfisher	*Ceryle alcyon*	RB
Red-headed Woodpecker	*Melanerpes erythrocephalus*	RB
Red-bellied Woodpecker	*Melanerpes carolinus*	RB
Yellow-bellied Sapsucker	*Sphyrapicus varius*	WV
Downy Woodpecker	*Picoides pubescens*	RB
Hairy Woodpecker	*Picoides villosus*	RB
Red-cockaded Woodpecker	*Picoides borealis*	RB
Northern Flicker	*Colaptes auratus*	RB
Pileated Woodpecker	*Dryocopus pileatus*	RB
Eastern Wood-pewee	*Contopus virens*	PM
Acadian Flycatcher	*Empidonax virescens*	MB Pm
Willow Flycatcher	*Empidonax traillii*	PM
Least Flycatcher	*Empidonax minimus*	PM WV
Eastern Phoebe	*Sayornis phoebe*	WV
Vermillion Flycatcher	*Pyrocephalus rubinus*	AV
Great Crested flycatcher	*Myiarchus crinitus*	MB WV
Western Kingbird	*Tyrannus verticalis*	WV
Eastern Kingbird	*Tyrannus tyrannus*	MB
Grey Kingbird	*Tyrannus dominicensis*	MB
Scissor-tailed Flycatcher	*Tyrannus forficatus*	WV
Purple Martin	*Progne subis*	MB
Tree Swallow	*Tachycineta bicolor*	WV PM
Northern Rough-winged Swallow	*Stelgidopteryx serripennis*	PM MB
Bank Swallow	*Riparia riparia*	PM
Cliff Swallow	*Hirundo pyrrhonota*	PM MB
Cave Swallow	*Hirundo fulva*	RB
Barn Swallow	*Hirundo rustica*	PM MB
Blue Jay	*Cyanocitta cristata*	RB
Florida Scrub-jay	*Aphelocoma coerulescens*	RB
American Crow	*Corvus brachyrhynchos*	RB
Fish Crow	*Corvus ossifragus*	RB
Carolina Chickadee	*Parus carolinensis*	RB
Tufted Titmouse	*Parus bicolor*	RB
Red-breasted Nuthatch	*Sitta canadensis*	WV
White-breasted Nuthatch	*Sitta carolinensis*	RB
Brown-headed Nuthatch	*Sitta pusilla*	RB
Brown Creeper	Certhia americana	WV
Red-whiskered Bulbul (SE Miami)*	*Pycnonotus jocosus*	RB
Carolina Wren	*Thryothorus ludovicianus*	RB
House Wren	*Troglodytes aedon*	WV
Winter Wren	*Troglodytes troglodytes*	WV
Sedge Wren	*Cistothorus platensis*	WV

English name	Scientific name	Status
Marsh Wren	*Cistothorus palustris*	RB
Golden-crowned Kinglet	*Regulus satrapa*	WV
Ruby-crowned Kinglet	*Regulus calendula*	WV
Blue-grey Gnatcatcher	*Polioptila caerulea*	RB
Eastern Bluebird	*Sialia sialis*	RB
Veery	*Catharus fuscescens*	PM
Grey-cheeked Thrush	*Catharus minimus*	PM
Swainson's Thrush	*Catharus ustulatus*	PM
Hermit Thrush	*Catharus guttatus*	WV PM
Wood Thrush	*Hylocichla mustelina*	PM
American Robin	*Turdus migratorius*	WV
Grey Catbird	*Dumetella carolinensis*	WV
Northern Mockingbird	*Mimus polyglottos*	RB
Brown Thrasher	*Toxostoma rufum*	RB
American Pipit	*Anthus spinoletta*	WV
Cedar Waxwing	*Bombycilla cedrorum*	WV
Loggerhead Shrike	*Lanius ludovicianus*	RB
European Starling*	*Sturnus vulgaris*	RB
Hill Mynah (Miami area)*	*Gracula religiosa*	RB
Common Mynah (Miami & Gulf area)*	*Acridotheres tristis*	RB
Crested Mynah (Miami area)*	*Acridotheres cristatellus*	RB
White-eyed Vireo	*Vireo griseus*	RB
Solitary Vireo	Vireo solitarius	WV
Yellow-throated Vireo	*Vireo flavifrons*	MB PM
Philadelphia Vireo	*Vireo philadelphicus*	PM
Red-eyed Vireo	*Vireo olivaceus*	PM
Black-whiskered Vireo	*Vireo altiloquus*	MB
Blue-winged Warbler	*Vermivora pinus*	PM
Tennessee Warbler	*Vermivora peregrina*	PM
Orange-crowned Warbler	*Vermivora celata*	WV
Nashville Warbler	*Vermivora ruficapilla*	PM
Northern Parula	*Parula americana*	MB WV
Yellow Warbler	*Dendroica petechia*	WV MB
Chestnut-sided Warbler	*Dendroica pensylvanica*	PM
Magnolia Warbler	*Dendroica magnolia*	PM
Cape May Warbler	*Dendroica tigrina*	WV PM
Black-throated Blue Warbler	*Dendroica caerulescens*	PM
Yellow-rumped Warbler	*Dendroica coronata*	WV
Black-throated Green Warbler	*Dendroica virens*	PM
Blackburnian Warbler	*Dendroica fusca*	PM
Yellow-throated Warbler	*Dendroica dominica*	RB
Pine Warbler	*Dendroica pinus*	RB
Prairie Warbler	*Dendroica discolor*	RB
Palm Warbler	*Dendroica palmarum*	WV
Blackpoll Warbler	*Dendroica striata*	PM
Black and White Warbler	*Mniotilta varia*	WV PM
American Redstart	*Setophaga ruticilla*	WV PM
Prothonotary Warbler	*Prothonotaria citrea*	MB
Worm-eating Warbler	*Helmitheros vermivorus*	PM
Swainson's Warbler	*Limnothlypis swainsonii*	MB
Ovenbird	*Seiurus aurocapillus*	WV PM

English name	Scientific name	Status
Northern Waterthrush	*Seiurus noveboracensis*	WV PM
Louisiana Waterthrush	*Seiurus motacilla*	PM
Kentucky Warbler	*Oporornis formosus*	MB
Connecticut Warbler	*Oproornis agilis*	PM
Common Yellowthroat	*Geothlypis thrichas*	RB
Hooded Warbler	*Wilsonia citrina*	MB
Yellow-breasted Chat	*Icteria virens*	MB
Summer Tanager	*Piranga rubra*	MB
Scarlet Tanager	*Piranga olivacea*	PM
Northern Cardinal	*Cardinalis cardinalis*	RB
Rose-breasted Grosbeak	*Pheucticus ludovicianus*	PM
Blue Grosbeak	*Guiraca caerules*	WV PM
Indigo Bunting	*Passerina cyanea*	WV MB
Painted Bunting (nests NE only)	*Passerina ciris*	RB
Dickcissel	*Spiza americana*	WV
Eastern Towhee	*Pipilo erythrophthalmus*	RB
Bachman's Sparrow	*Aimophila aestivalis*	RB
Chipping Sparrow	*Spizella passerina*	WV
Field Sparrow	*Spizella pusilla*	WV
Vesper Sparrow	*Pooecetes gramineus*	WV
Savannah Sparrow	*Passerculus sandwichensis*	WV
Grasshopper Sparrow	*Ammodramus savannarum*	MB
Saltmarsh Sharp-tailed Sparrow	*Ammodramus caudacutus*	WV
Nelson's Sharp-tailed Sparrow	*Ammodramius nelsonii*	WV
Seaside Sparrow	*Ammodramus maritimus*	RB
Song Sparrow	*Melospiza melodia*	WV
Swamp Sparrow	*Melospiza georgiana*	WV
White-throated Sparrow	*Zonotrichia albicollis*	WV
White-crowned Sparrow	*Zonotrichia leucophrys*	PM
Dark-eyed Junco	*Junco hyemalis*	WV
Bobolink	*Dolichonyx oryzivorus*	PM
Red-winged Blackbird	*Agelaius phoeniceus*	RB
Eastern Meadowlark	*Sturnella magna*	RB
Yellow-headed Blackbird	*Xanthocephalus xanthocephalus*	AV
Rusty Blackbird	*Euphagus carolinus*	WV
Brewer's Blackbird	*Euphagus cyanocephalus*	WV
Boat-tailed Grackle	*Quiscalus major*	RB
Common Grackle	*Quiscalus quiscula*	RB
Shiny Cowbird	*Molothrus bonariensis*	AV
Bronzed Cowbird	*Molothrus aeneus*	AV
Brown-headed Cowbird	*Molothrus ater*	RB
Orchard Oriole	*Icterus spurius*	PM
Spot-breasted Oriole*	*Icterus pectoralis*	RB
Baltimore Oriole	*Icterus galbula*	WV PM
Pine Siskin	*Carduelis pinus*	WV
American Goldfinch	*Carduelis tristis*	WV
House Sparrow*	*Passer domesticus*	RB
Java Sparrow (Miami area)*	*Padda oryzivora*	RB

						English name	Scientific name	Status

Checklist of the Mammals of Florida

English and Scientific name	Status
Opossum *Didelphis virginiana*	Woodlands
Southeastern Shrew *Sorex longirostris*	Woods in north
Short-tailed Shrew *Blarina carolinensis*	Common
Least Shrew *Cryptotis parva*	Marshes & prairies
Eastern Mole *Scalopus aquaticusi*	Common on sandy soils
Cuban House Bat *Molossus molossus*	Middle & Lower Keys only
Little Brown Bat *Myotis lucifugus*	Panhandle & North
Grey Bat *Myotis grisescens*	Rare; North-east
Southeastern Bat *Myotis austroriparius*	Panhandle & North
Silver-haired Bat *Lasionycteris noctivagans*	Panhandle woods
Eastern Pipistrelle *Pipistrellus subflavus*	North & Central caves
Rafinesque's Big-eared Bat *Plecotus rafinesquii*	North & Central woods
Big Brown Bat *Eptesicus fuscus*	North & Central caves
Hoary Bat *Lasiurus cinereus*	North & Central woods
Red Bat *Lasiurus borealis*	North & Panhandle woods
Seminole Bat *Lasiurus seminolus*	North & Central woods
Yellow Bat *Lasiurus intermedius*	Woodlands
Evening Bat *Nycticeius humeralis*	Common everywhere
Brazilian Free-tailed Bat *Tadarida brasiliensis*	Common throughout
Mastiff Bat *Eumops glaucinus*	Miami area only
Nine-banded Armadillo *Dasypus novemcinctus*	Sandy woodlands
Eastern Cottontail *Sylvilagus floridanus*	Woodlands except Keys
Marsh Rabbit *Sylvilagus palustris*	Marshes throughout
Eastern Chipmunk *Tamias striatus*	Western Panhandle only
Grey Squirrel *Scurius carolinensis*	Woodlands throughout
Fox Squirrel *Scurius niger*	Uncommon in woodlands
Red-bellied Squirrel *Scurius aureogaster*	Mainly Elliot Key
Southern Flying Squirrel *Glaucomys volans*	Woodlands
Southeastern Pocket Gopher *Geomys pinetis*	North & Central
Beaver *Castor canadensis*	Panhandle only
Eastern Woodrat *Neotoma floridana*	Key Large, North-central
Hispid Cotton Rat *Sigmodon hispidus*	Wetlands throughout
Eastern Harvest Mouse *Reithrodontomys humulis*	North & Central
Marsh Rice Rat *Oryzomys palustris*	Marshes throughout
Florida Mouse *Podomys floriadanus*	Rare endemic; Central
Oldfield Mouse *Peromyscus polionotus*	North & Central
Cotton Mouse *Peromyscus gossypinus*	Common in scrub
Golden Mouse *Ochrotomys nuttalli*	North & Central only
Pine Vole *Microtus pinetorum*	Panhandle & North pines
Round-tailed Muskrat *Neofiber alleni*	Marshes throughout
House Mouse *Mus musculus*	Introduced; common
Black Rat *Rattus rattus*	Introduced; common
Brown Rat *Rattus norvegicus*	Introduced; common
Coypu *Myocastor coypus*	Introduced; some marshes
Black Bear *Ursus americanus*	Scattered forests
Raccoon *Procyon lotor*	Woodlands
Mink *Mustela vison*	Wet woodlands
Long-tailed Weasel *Mustela frenata*	North & Central only
Striped Skunk *Mephitis mephitis*	Woodlands & prairies

English and Scientific name	Status
Spotted Skunk *Spilogale putorius*	Woodlands & priaries
River Otter *Lutra canadenis*	Streams & Lakes
Grey Fox *Urocyon cinereoargenteus*	Open woodlands
Red Fox *Vulpes vulpes*	Introduced; increasing
Coyote *Canis latrans*	Woodlands; increasing
Bobcat *Lynx rufus*	Woodlands
Mountain Lion *Felis concolor*	Extremely rare
Atlantic Bottle-nosed Dolphin *Tursiops truncatus*	Common off both coasts
West Indian Manatee *Trichecus manatus*	Rare & decreasing
White-tailed Deer *Odocoileus virginianus*	Woodlands
Key Deer *Odocoileus virginianus clavium*	Small endemic race of White-tailed Deer

In addition wild pigs of domestic origin are found in feral populations in many marshy areas. As with most wildlife in Florida there are many more exotic escapes and releases which may be encountered.

Checklist of the Amphibians of Florida

Found throughout the state unless otherwise noted.

English and Scientific name	Status
Gulf Coast Waterdog *Necturus beyeri*	Panhandle
Two-toed Amphiuma *Amphiuma means*	
One-toed Amphiuma *Amphiuma pholeter*	Panhandle & Gulf Coast
Greater Siren *Siren lacertina*	
Lesser Siren *Siren intermedia*	
Dwarf Siren *Pseudobranchus striatus*	
Mole Salamander *Ambystoma talpoideum*	Panhandle to Central
Marbled Salamander *Ambystoma opacum*	Panhandle & North
Flatwoods Salamander *Ambystoma cingulatum*	Panhandle & North
Tiger Salamander *Ambystoma tigrinum*	Panhandle to Central
Spotted Newt *Notophthalmus viridescens*	
Striped Newt *Notophthalmus perstriatus*	North & Central
Northern Dusky Salamander *Desmognathus fuscus*	Panhandle to Central
Southern Dusky Salamander *Desmognathus auriculatus*	Absent from South
Slimy Salamander *Plethodon glutinosus*	Absent from South
Four-toed Salamander *Hemidactylium scutatum*	Panhandle
Many-lined Salamander *Sterochilus marginatus*	Okefenokee Swamp
Mud Salamander *Pseudotriton montanus*	Absent from South
Red Salamander *Pseudotriton ruber*	Panhandle
Two-lined Salamander *Eurycea bislineata*	Panhandle
Long-tailed Salamander *Eurycea longicauda*	Panhandle
Dwarf Salamander *Eurycea quadridigitata*	Absent from South
Georgia Blind Salamander *Haideotriton wallacei*	Marianna area only
Eastern Spadefoot Toad *Scaphiopus holbrooki*	
Southern Toad *Bufo terrestris*	
Woodhouse's Toad *Bufo woodhousei*	Panhandle
Oak Toad *Bufo quercicus*	
Giant Toad *Bufo marinus*	Introduced: Not in North
Greenhouse Frog *Eleutherodactylus planirostris*	Introduced
Southern Cricket Frog *Acris gryllus*	
Northern Cricket Frog *Acris crepitans*	Panhandle
Spring Peeper *Hyla crucifer*	Absent from South
Pine Barrens Treefrog *Hyla andersoni*	Western Panhandle
Green Treefrog *Hyla cinerea*	
Barking Treefrog *Hyla gratiosa*	Absent from extreme South
Pine Woods Treefrog *Hyla femoralis*	Absent from extreme South
Squirrel Treefrog *Hyla squirella*	
Grey Treefrog *Hyla chrysoscelis*	Panhandle & North
Bird-voiced Treefrog *Hyla avivoca*	Panhandle
Cuban Treefrog *Osteopilus septentrionalis*	Introduced: Not in North
Southern Chorus Frog *Pseudacris nigrita*	Absent from extreme South
Ornate Chorus Frog *Pseudacris ornata*	Absent in South
Little Grass Frog *Pseudacris ocularis*	
Eastern Narrowmouth Toad *Gastrophyne crolinensis*	
Bullfrog *Rana catesbeiana*	Absent from South
River Frog *Rana heckscheri*	Absent from South
Pig Frog *Rana grylio*	
Carpenter Frog *Rana virgatipes*	Okefenokee Swamp

English name	Scientific name	Status
Bronze Frog	*Rana clamitans*	Panhandle & North
Southern Leopard Frog	*Rana utricularia*	
Gopher Frog	*Rana capito*	
Florida Bog Frog	*Rana okaloosae*	Endemic; Yellow & East Bay Rivers

Checklist of the Reptiles of Florida

Found throughout the state unless otherwise noted. **P = Poisonous Snake**

English and Scientific name	Status
American Crocodile *Crocodylus acutus*	Rare; extreme South
American Alligator *Alligator mississippiensis*	
Brown Caiman *Caiman crocodilus*	Introduced; Miami area
Common Snapping Turtle *Chelydra serpentina*	
Alligator Snapping Turtle *Macroclemys temmincki*	Panhandle & North-west
Common Musk Turtle *Sternotherus odoratus*	
Loggerhead Musk Turtle *Sternotherus minor*	Absent from South
Mud Turtle *Kinosternon subrubrum*	
Striped Mud Turtle *Kinosternon bauri*	Absent from NW Panhandle
Spotted Turtle *Clemmys guttata*	North & South
Box Turtle *Terrapene carolina*	
Diamondback Terrapin *Melaclemys terrapin*	Marshes & mangroves
Barbour's Map Turtle *Graptemys barbouri*	Panhandle
Alabama Map Turtle *Graptemys pulchra*	Western Panhandle
Red-eared Slider *Trachemys scripta*	Panhandle & North
River Cooter *Pseudemys concinna*	Gulf coast to Tampa Bay
Peninsula Cooter *Pseudemys floridana*	Absent from South
Florida Redbelly Turtle *Pseudemys nelsoni*	Endemic to Florida
Alabama Redbelly Turtle *Pseudemys alabamensis*	Panhandle
Chicken Turtle *Deirochelys reticularia*	
Gopher Tortoise *Gopherus polyphemus*	
Green Turtle *Chelonia mydas*	Atlantic coast only
Loggerhead Turtle *Caretta caretta*	Coastal
Leatherback Turtle *Dermochelys coriacea*	Scarce on Atlantic coast
Smooth Softshell *Apalone muticus*	Western Panhandle
Spiny Softshell *Apalone spiniferus*	Panhandle
Florida Softshell *Apalone ferox*	
Tropical House Gecko *Hemidactylus mabouia*	Introduced; South
Fox Gecko *Hemidactylus frenatus*	Introduced; South
Mediterranean Gecko *Hemidactylus turcicus*	Introduced
Indo-Pacific Gecko *Hemidactylus garnoti*	Introduced
Ashy Gecko *Sphaerodactylus elegans*	Introduced; Lower Keys
Florida Reef Gecko *Sphaerodactylus notatus*	Extreme South
Ocellated Gecko *Sphaerodactylus argus*	Introduced; Key West
Yellow-headed Gecko *Gonatodes albogularis*	Introduced; Key West
Tokay Gecko *Gekko gekko*	Introduced
Green Anole *Anolis carolinensis*	
Brown Anole *Anolis sagrei*	Introduced
Jamaican Giant Anole *Anolis garmani*	Introduced; Miami
Crested Anole *Anolis cristatellus*	Introduced; Miami
Large-headed Anole *Anolis cybotes*	Introduced; Miami & F. Lauderdale
Bark Anole *Anolis distichus*	Introduced; SE & Keys
Knight Anole *Anolis equestris*	Introduced; Miami & F. Lauderdale
Brown Basilisk Basilicus vittatus	Introduced; Miami area
Green Iguana *Iguana iguana*	Introduced; Miami & South
Spiny-tailed Iguana *Ctenosaura pectinata*	Introduced; Miami
Eastern Fence Lizard *Sceloporus undulatus*	Absent from south

English name	Scientific name	Status
Florida Scrub Lizard	*Sceloporus woodi*	Endemic to South coast
Texas Horned Lizard	*Phrynosoma cornutum*	Introduced; Pensecola
Curly-tailed Lizard	*Leiocephalus carinatus*	Introduced; South-east
Six-lined Racerunner	*Cnemidophorus sexlineatus*	
Tropical Racerunner	*Cnemidophorus lemniscatus*	Introduced; Miami
Ground Lizard	*Ameiva ameiva*	Introduced; Miami
Ground Skink	*Scincella lateralis*	
Northern Five-lined Skink	*Eumeces fasciatus*	Panhandle & North
Broad-headed Skink	*Eumeces laticeps*	Panhandle & North
Southeastern Five-lined Skink	*Eumeces inexpectatus*	
Coal Skink	*Eumeces anthracinus*	Central Panhandle
Mole Skink	*Eumeces egregius*	
Sand Skink	*Neoseps reynoldsi*	Endemic Central
Eastern Glass Lizard	*Ophisaurus ventralis*	
Slender glass Lizard	*Ophisaurus attenuatus*	
Island Glass Lizard	*Ophisaurus compressus*	
Mimic Glass Lizard	*Ophisaurus mimicus*	Panhandle & North-east
Worm Lizard	*Rhineura floridana*	Endemic south to Okeechobee
Brahminy Blind Snake	*Ramphotyphlops braminus*	Introduced; Central & South
Green Water Snake	*Nerodia floridana*	
Brown Water Snake	*Nerodia taxispilota*	
Water Snake	*Nerodia fasciata*	
Salt-Marsh Snake	*Nerodia clarkii*	
Black Swamp Snake	*Seminatrix pygaea*	
Brown Snake	*Storeria dekayi*	
Red-bellied Snake	*Storeria occipitomaculata*	South & Central
Red-bellied Water Snake	*Nerodia erythrogaster*	Panhandle & North
Midland Water Snake	*Nerodia sipedon*	Western Panhandle
Queen Snake	*Regina septemvittata*	Panhandle
Glossy Water Snake	*Regina rigida*	Absent in South
Striped Crayfish Snake	*Regina alleni*	
Garter Snake	*Thamnophis sirtalis*	
Ribbon Snake	*Thamnophis sauritus*	
Smooth Earth Snake	*Virginia valeriae*	
Rough Earth Snake	*Virginia striatula*	Absent in South
Eastern Hognose Snake	*Heterodon platyrhinos*	
Southern Hognose Snake	*Heterodon simus*	Absent in South
Ringneck Snake	*Diadophis punctatus*	
Pinewoods Snake	*Rhadinaea flavilata*	
Eastern Mud Snake	Farancia abacura	
Rainbow Snake	*Farancia erytrogramma*	Absent in South
Black Racer	*Coluber constrictor*	
Eastern Coachwhip	*Masticophis flagellum*	
Rough Green Snake	*Opheodrys aestivus*	
Indigo Snake	*Drymarchon corais*	
Corn Snake	*Elaphe guttata*	
Rat Snake	*Elaphe obsoleta*	
Pine Snake	*Pituophis melanoleucus*	Absent south of Okeechobee
Common Kingsnake	*Lampropeltis getulus*	
Scarlet Kingsnake	*Lampropeltis triangulum*	

English name	Scientific name	Status
Mole Snake	*Lampropeltis calligaster*	Panhandle & Central
Scarlet Snake	*Cemophora coccinea*	
Short-tailed Snake	*Stilosoma extenuatum*	Endemic in North
Crowned Snake	*Tantilla relicta*	
Rim-Rock Crowned Snake	*Tantilla oolitica*	Endemic Dade Co. & Keys
Southeastern Crowned Snake	*Tantilla coronata*	Panhandle
Coral Snake	*Micrurus fulvius* P	
Copperhead	*Agkistrodon contortrix* P	Panhandle
Cottonmouth	*Agkistrodon piscivorus* P	
Dusky Pigmy Rattlesnake	*Sistrurus miliarius* P	
Timber Rattlesnake	*Crotalus horridus* P	Central North
Eastern Diamondback Rattlesnake	*Crotalus adamanteus* P	

Recommended Reading including Field Guides

A Birder's Guide to Florida. W. Pranty - American Birding Association 1996.

Birds of South Florida. Connie Toops and Willard E. Dilley - River Road Press 1986.

Field Guide to the Birds of North America, 2nd Ed. - National Geographic.

A Field Guide to the Birds East of the Rockies. Roger Tory Peterson - Houghton Mifflin.

National Audubon Society Field Guide to North American Birds, Revised Ed. - Knopf 1995.

Peterson Field Guide to Mammals, William H. Burt & Richard P. Grossenheider - Houghton Mifflin

Peterson Field Guide to Reptiles & Amphibians, Eastern/Central North America, Roger Conant, Joseph T. Collins - Houghton Mifflin

NOTES

NOTES